Mastering AI Agent Development with Python

Written By

Morgan Devline

Title: Mastering AI Agent Development with Python

Author: Morgan Devline

Table of Content

Chapter 1: Introduction to AI Agents

1.1 What Are AI Agents?

AI agents are autonomous software programs designed to perform tasks, make decisions, and adapt to their environments using artificial intelligence techniques. These entities operate independently, perceiving their surroundings—whether digital data, user inputs, or sensor readings—and acting to achieve specific goals without constant human oversight. By leveraging methods like machine learning, natural language processing, and decision-making algorithms, AI agents can learn from experience, refine their behavior, and tackle everything from simple automation to complex problem-solving. In essence, they're the backbone of intelligent systems, driving efficiency and innovation across industries as of 2025.

Defining Characteristics

AI agents stand out due to a set of core traits that define their functionality:

- **Autonomy**: They work without needing step-by-step human guidance, executing tasks based on their programming and learned insights. For example, a virtual assistant can schedule meetings by analyzing your calendar independently.

- **Reactivity**: They respond to changes in their environment, adjusting actions in real-time. A chatbot, for instance, shifts its replies based on a user's tone or question.

- **Proactivity**: Beyond reacting, many agents anticipate needs and act preemptively—like a maintenance bot predicting equipment failure and scheduling repairs before a breakdown occurs.

- **Learning**: They improve over time by analyzing data and outcomes, using techniques like reinforcement learning to get smarter with each interaction.

- **Collaboration**: In multi-agent setups, they coordinate with other agents, sharing information to solve problems, such as a team of bots managing traffic flow in a smart city.

These traits make AI agents versatile, capable of operating in dynamic, unpredictable settings where rigid scripts fall short.

Types of AI Agents

AI agents range from basic to highly sophisticated, depending on their complexity and purpose:

- **Simple Agents**: These are narrowly focused, handling specific tasks with predefined rules or basic AI. A classic example is a chatbot that answers FAQs—like "What's your shipping policy?"—using a fixed set of responses. Another is a recommendation system suggesting products based on past purchases, relying on straightforward pattern recognition.

- **Complex Agents**: These go further, integrating advanced learning, reasoning, and adaptability. Virtual assistants like Siri or Alexa process natural language, manage schedules, and adapt to user habits. Autonomous vehicles, such as Tesla's self-driving cars, navigate roads by interpreting sensor data in real-time. In 2025, complex agents also include multi-modal systems that handle text, images, and audio—like a bot that reads a product photo and describes it—or emotionally intelligent agents that adjust responses based on a user's mood, detected through voice or word choice.

Evolution and Importance

AI agents have come a long way from their origins as rule-based systems, where hard-coded instructions limited them to repetitive tasks like factory automation. Advances in computing power, data availability, and AI techniques—especially deep learning and large language models—have transformed them into dynamic tools. By 2025, they're tackling nuanced challenges, from diagnosing diseases to generating creative content. This evolution has made them critical across industries: customer service bots cut response times, healthcare agents improve diagnostic accuracy, and autonomous systems revolutionize transportation. Their ability to automate, optimize, and innovate is reshaping how businesses operate and how we interact with technology daily.

Relevance to Development

Understanding AI agents is the first step to mastering their creation, which is what this book is all about. Whether it's a simple bot answering questions or a complex system coordinating logistics, agents rely on the same principles—perception, reasoning, action—that you'll learn to implement with Python. Their growing presence in 2025, handling up to 70% of customer queries or boosting productivity by 30% in some firms, underscores their value. This section sets the stage for diving into Python's tools and techniques, starting with a customer support bot project that will grow from a basic script into a real-world-ready solution, showing you how to harness these capabilities firsthand.

AI agents are more than software—they're intelligent, adaptable systems that bridge human needs and technological potential. From simple task-runners to proactive problem-solvers, they're defined by autonomy, learning, and collaboration, with an evolution that's made them indispensable. As you move through this book, you'll see how to build them, tapping into their power to automate, assist, and innovate in ways that matter today and tomorrow.

1.2 Applications of AI Agents

AI agents are reshaping industries and daily life by automating tasks, making decisions, and adapting to diverse needs with remarkable efficiency. Their applications span a wide range of fields, from customer service to healthcare, finance, autonomous systems, education, creative industries, security, workplace automation, and scientific research. In 2025, these agents are not only reacting to commands but also proactively anticipating needs, such as scheduling meetings or predicting equipment failures, making them indispensable tools for managing complex, large-scale operations. This versatility is driving a transformation in how businesses function, how services are delivered, and even how creative and intellectual work is approached.

Functional Categories and Examples

AI agents can be grouped into functional categories based on the types of tasks they perform, each with practical examples that highlight their real-world impact:

- **Conversational Agents**: These agents engage with users through natural language, answering questions and providing assistance. For instance, virtual assistants like Siri and Alexa handle everyday queries, while customer service chatbots on platforms like Amazon's help desk resolve up to 70% of inquiries without human intervention, streamlining support and cutting response times.

- **Recommendation Agents**: These analyse user behaviour to suggest tailored options. Netflix uses them to recommend movies based on viewing history, and Amazon employs them to suggest products, boosting sales by anticipating customer preferences with precision.

- **Task Automation Agents**: This handle repetitive or routine tasks to save time and effort. Tools like Zapier automate workflows by connecting apps, while Microsoft Cortana schedules meetings by scanning calendars and suggesting optimal times, enhancing productivity.

- **Decision-Making Agents**: These assist in complex decision processes by analyzing data and providing insights. In finance, algorithmic trading bots execute trades based on market trends, and IBM's Watson for Oncology evaluates patient data to recommend cancer treatments, supporting doctors with evidence-based options.

- **Creative Agents**: These generate original content, pushing boundaries in artistic fields. Systems like DALL-E create detailed images from text prompts, and GPT-3 composes music or writes stories, offering tools for artists and writers to explore new creative avenues.

- **Simulation Agents**: These model scenarios for training or research. In video games, AI opponents adapt to player strategies, while scientific simulations model climate patterns or chemical reactions, accelerating discovery without real-world risks.

- **Monitoring and Alerting Agents**: These watch systems for anomalies and issue alerts. Cybersecurity agents detect hacking attempts by spotting unusual network activity, and environmental monitors track air quality, notifying authorities of hazardous changes.

Industry-Specific Applications

Beyond functional roles, AI agents are tailored to specific industries, solving unique challenges and driving innovation:

- **Healthcare**: AI agents monitor patient vitals, predict disease progression, and assist with diagnostics. Virtual health advisors track chronic conditions like diabetes, alerting patients to medication needs, while systems like Watson analyze medical records to suggest treatment plans, improving accuracy and speed in care delivery.

- **Finance**: They detect fraud, assess risks, and manage investments. By 2025, nearly triple the current 18% of organizations are expected to use AI for fraud detection, analyzing transactions in real-time to flag suspicious patterns, while trading agents optimize portfolios based on market shifts.

- **Autonomous Systems**: AI agents power self-driving cars, drones, and robotics. Tesla's Autopilot navigates roads by processing sensor data to avoid obstacles, and delivery drones map routes, transforming transportation and logistics with safe, efficient automation.

- **Education**: They personalize learning by adapting to student needs. Platforms like Duolingo adjust lessons based on performance, offering tailored exercises to improve language skills, making education more engaging and effective.

- **Research and Development**: AI agents analyze vast datasets and test hypotheses, speeding up scientific progress. In drug discovery, they sift through molecular data to identify promising compounds, cutting development time from years to months, as seen in genomics research.

Emerging Trends in 2025

As of 2025, AI agents are evolving beyond reactive tools into proactive problem-solvers. They anticipate needs—like suggesting meeting times or predicting equipment maintenance—rather than waiting for instructions. This shift is evident in workplace automation, where agents manage schedules and optimize workflows, and in industries like healthcare, where they forecast patient outcomes. Companies like Salesforce report a 30% productivity boost from these agents, with some even reducing hiring of software engineers due to their efficiency. This proactive capability is also tackling large-scale challenges, such as managing thousands of customer interactions or optimizing supply chains, reshaping business operations and workforce dynamics.

Impact and Relevance

The applications of AI agents are vast and growing, driven by their ability to handle both mundane and sophisticated tasks. They're reducing costs, improving accuracy, and opening new possibilities, from automating customer support to revolutionizing creative expression. For developers, understanding these applications is key to building agents that meet real-world demands. Later chapters will explore how to create these agents using Python, turning these examples into practical projects, such as designing a chatbot or a recommendation system, empowering you to master their development.

AI agents are not just tools but game-changers across industries. Whether it's a chatbot easing customer frustrations, a car driving itself, or a system crafting art, their applications show their power to enhance efficiency and innovation. As we move through this book, you'll see how to harness this potential, building agents that can transform the world around you.

1.3 Why Python for AI Agent Development?

Python has emerged as the go-to language for AI agent development, blending simplicity, power, and versatility in a way that few other languages can match. Its straightforward syntax makes it easy to learn and use, allowing developers to focus on crafting intelligent agents rather than wrestling with complex code structures. Beyond ease, Python boasts a vast ecosystem of libraries and tools tailored for AI, a thriving community offering endless support, and seamless integration with cutting-edge frameworks and platforms. As of 2025, these qualities make Python not just a practical choice but a powerhouse for building everything from simple chatbots to sophisticated multi-agent systems.

Simplicity and Readability

Python's clean and concise syntax is a standout feature, making it accessible to beginners while remaining efficient for seasoned developers. Unlike languages with steeper learning curves, Python lets you write code that's easy to read and maintain—crucial when designing AI agents with intricate logic. For example, a basic agent that processes user input can be written in just a few lines, freeing you to concentrate on refining its intelligence rather than debugging syntax errors. This simplicity accelerates prototyping and experimentation, key steps in AI development where ideas need quick testing and iteration.

Rich Ecosystem of Libraries and Tools

Python's strength lies in its extensive collection of libraries, purpose-built for AI tasks. Libraries like TensorFlow and PyTorch power machine learning models, enabling agents to learn from data and make predictions. Scikit-learn offers tools for simpler algorithms, perfect for quick agent prototypes, while NumPy and Pandas handle data manipulation with ease. For AI agents specifically, LangChain provides a framework to integrate memory and tools, and Hugging Face delivers pre-trained models for natural language processing and beyond. These libraries aren't just add-ons—they're robust, well-documented resources that slash development time and boost capability, letting you build agents that process text, images, or even audio with minimal setup.

Thriving Community and Support

Python's massive, active community is a goldmine for developers. Thousands of contributors worldwide maintain libraries, share tutorials, and solve problems on forums, ensuring you're never stuck. Need to debug an agent's decision-making logic? A quick search yields code snippets, explanations, and best practices from experts. This support network is especially valuable in 2025, as AI evolves rapidly—community updates keep Python's tools cutting-edge, from new model architectures to optimized deployment strategies. Whether you're a solo coder or part of a team, this collective knowledge base accelerates learning and troubleshooting.

Compatibility with AI Frameworks

Python shines in its compatibility with leading AI frameworks, making it a flexible foundation for agent development. Frameworks like CrewAI enable multi-agent collaboration, Microsoft Semantic Kernel integrates enterprise-grade AI, and AutoGen supports automated agent design—all seamlessly tied to Python. This compatibility means you can build a simple FAQ bot or a complex system where agents coordinate tasks, all within the same language. Python's ability to bridge these frameworks ensures you're not locked into one approach, giving you freedom to adapt as project needs evolve.

Integration with Cloud Platforms

In today's world, deploying AI agents at scale is critical, and Python excels here too. It integrates smoothly with cloud platforms like Amazon Web Services (AWS), Google Cloud, and Microsoft Azure, offering tools to host agents, manage data, and scale performance. For instance, using Python with AWS Lambda, you can deploy a customer support agent that handles thousands of queries daily, with minimal overhead. This cloud compatibility makes Python practical for real-world applications, where agents must run reliably and grow with demand, a necessity highlighted by 2025's focus on scalable automation.

Cross-Platform and Scalability

Python's cross-platform nature lets you develop agents on Windows, macOS, or Linux without major rewrites, a boon for testing and deployment across diverse environments. Its scalability shines through as well—start with a small agent on a local machine, then scale it to a distributed cloud system handling massive workloads. This flexibility is key for AI agents, which might begin as prototypes but grow into enterprise solutions, such as a fraud detection system processing millions of transactions.

Industry Adoption and Proven Track Record

Python isn't just popular—it's the backbone of AI in industry. Tech giants like Google, Amazon, and Tesla rely on it for AI projects, from search algorithms to autonomous driving. Startups and research labs alike adopt Python for its proven ability to deliver results, whether in healthcare diagnostics or creative content generation. By 2025, its dominance is clear: companies report productivity gains—like a 30% boost in software development tasks—thanks to Python-based AI agents. This widespread use validates its reliability and ensures a wealth of real-world examples to learn from.

Why It Matters for This Book

Python's strengths make it the ideal choice for mastering AI agent development in this book. Its simplicity lets you dive into coding agents without a steep learning curve, while its libraries and frameworks provide the tools to build anything from a basic chatbot to a multi-modal agent handling text, images, and audio. The community support ensures you'll find solutions as you progress, and its cloud integration and scalability prepare you for real-world deployment. Later chapters will leverage these advantages, guiding you through hands-on projects—like creating a customer support bot—using Python's full potential to turn concepts into working agents.

Python stands out for AI agent development because it combines ease, power, and practicality in a way that empowers developers. Its readable code, rich libraries, strong community, framework compatibility, cloud integration, scalability, and industry trust make it unmatched. As you embark on this journey to master AI agents, Python will be your reliable companion, simplifying the complex and amplifying your ability to innovate.

1.4 Overview of the Book

"Mastering AI Agent Development with Python" is your comprehensive guide to designing, building, and deploying AI agents—autonomous programs that leverage artificial intelligence to perform tasks, make decisions, and adapt to their environments. This book takes you from the fundamentals to advanced techniques, equipping you with the knowledge and hands-on skills to create agents that solve real-world problems. Whether you're an intermediate programmer looking to break into AI or an advanced developer aiming to refine your expertise, this book offers a structured path to mastery, grounded in Python's powerful capabilities. As of 2025, with AI agents transforming industries, this journey is both timely and practical, blending theory with actionable projects to ensure you can build agents that work.

Purpose and Audience

The purpose of this book is to demystify AI agent development, making it accessible and actionable through Python, the leading language for AI in 2025. It's designed for intermediate to advanced programmers who know basic Python and want to harness AI to create intelligent systems—think chatbots that anticipate customer needs, recommendation engines that personalize suggestions, or multi-agent teams managing complex workflows. You don't need a PhD in machine learning, but a curiosity for AI and a willingness to experiment will carry you far. By the end, you'll have the tools to craft agents for industries like healthcare, finance, or even creative fields, turning ideas into functional solutions.

Structure and Flow

The book is organized into 13 chapters, each building on the last to take you from beginner concepts to cutting-edge applications. Here's how it unfolds:

- **Chapter 1: Introduction to AI Agents**: You're here—learning what AI agents are, their applications, and why Python is your tool of choice, setting the stage for everything to come.

- **Chapter 2: Setting Up the Development Environment**: Get hands-on with installing Python, key libraries like LangChain, and configuring your workspace, ensuring you're ready to code.

- **Chapter 3: Understanding AI Agent Frameworks**: Explore frameworks like CrewAI and AutoGen, dissecting their components—LLMs, prompts, tools—so you can choose the right one for your agent.

- **Chapter 4: Building Basic AI Agents with LangChain**: Write your first agent using the ReAct pattern, defining actions and handling inputs, with exercises to test your skills.

- **Chapter 5: Advanced Agent Development**: Dive deeper into memory management, decision-making, and customization, turning simple agents into sophisticated ones.

- **Chapter 6: Multi-Agent Systems**: Learn to design agents that collaborate, like a team solving logistics problems, with practical examples of coordination.

- **Chapter 7: Integrating with External Services**: Connect agents to APIs like Slack or scrape web data securely, making them interact with the real world.

- **Chapter 8: Training and Optimizing AI Agents**: Master training techniques like reinforcement learning, evaluate performance, and fine-tune for specific tasks.

- **Chapter 9: Testing and Debugging AI Agents**: Build reliable agents with strategies to test functionality and fix bugs, ensuring they perform as intended.

- **Chapter 10: Deploying AI Agents**: Take agents live on cloud platforms like AWS, setting up scalable systems with continuous deployment.

- **Chapter 11: Ethical Considerations in AI Agent Development**: Tackle bias, privacy, and responsible design, preparing you to build trustworthy agents.

- **Chapter 12: Real-World Use Cases**: Study agents in action— customer support, data analysis—and design your own for specific industries.

- **Chapter 13: Emerging Trends and Future Directions**: Explore 2025 trends like multi-modal agents and no-code development, keeping you ahead of the curve.

Each chapter ends with exercises—like tweaking an agent's logic or integrating a new tool—reinforcing what you've learned through practice.

The Sample Project: Building a Customer Support Bot

A unique feature of this book is a running sample project: creating a customer support bot. Introduced here, this project evolves across chapters, starting with a basic chatbot in Chapter 4 that answers FAQs. By Chapter 5, it gains memory to remember past interactions; in Chapter 6, it collaborates with other agents to escalate issues; and by Chapter 10, it's deployed on the cloud, handling real customer queries. This hands-on thread ties the book together, letting you apply concepts step-by-step to a tangible outcome. You'll brainstorm its requirements in Chapter 1's exercises, setting the foundation for a practical learning experience that mirrors real-world development.

Learning Approach

This book balances theory and practice, ensuring you understand *why* agents work while mastering *how* to build them. Each chapter starts with clear explanations—say, how memory enhances agent performance—followed by Python code examples you can run and tweak. Exercises at the end, like optimizing an agent's response time, push you to experiment, while the sample project provides a continuous challenge. The focus is on doing, not just reading, so you'll write code, test it, and refine it, building confidence as you go. By 2025 standards, this approach aligns with the demand for practical AI skills, preparing you for both personal projects and professional roles.

What You'll Gain

By the end, you'll have a deep understanding of AI agent development and the ability to create them with Python. You'll know how to set up a robust environment, leverage frameworks like LangChain, and build agents that learn, collaborate, and scale. You'll tackle real-world challenges—like deploying a bot for thousands of users—while navigating ethical pitfalls like bias. The sample project will leave you with a working customer support bot, a portfolio piece to showcase your skills. Beyond that, you'll be ready to explore 2025's frontiers, from multi-modal agents handling images and text to proactive systems predicting user needs.

Why This Matters in 2025

AI agents are everywhere in 2025—automating workflows, enhancing customer experiences, and even shaping creative industries. Companies report productivity boosts of 30% or more, with some rethinking hiring due to agent efficiency. This book positions you to ride this wave, giving you the tools to build agents that meet these demands. Whether you're automating a small business task or designing a system for a tech giant, the skills here are your entry point to a field that's redefining technology.

"Mastering AI Agent Development with Python" is more than a textbook—it's a hands-on journey to becoming an AI agent expert. With a clear structure, practical exercises, and a real-world project, it bridges the gap between theory and application. As you turn these pages, you'll not only learn how AI agents work but also build them yourself, ready to innovate in a world where they're increasingly vital. Let's dive in and start creating.

1.5 Introduction to Sample Project: Building a Customer Support Bot

The heart of this book lies in a hands-on sample project: designing, building, and deploying a customer support bot using Python. This project is your chance to apply everything you'll learn, from crafting a basic chatbot to creating a sophisticated, cloud-deployed agent that handles real customer interactions. Starting as a simple tool to answer FAQs, it will evolve across the chapters into a proactive, multi-functional system—complete with memory, collaboration capabilities, and scalability. By the end, you'll have a working bot that showcases your skills and mirrors real-world applications, making this not just a learning exercise but a practical achievement you can build on.

What Is the Customer Support Bot?

Imagine a bot that sits on a company's website or app, ready to assist customers 24/7. At its core, this customer support bot answers common questions—like "What's your return policy?" or "How do I reset my password?"—using natural language understanding. But it's more than a static FAQ reader. As you progress through the book, it will gain abilities like remembering past chats, escalating complex issues to other agents, and even suggesting solutions before customers ask. By 2025, such bots are standard in industries like e-commerce, tech support, and hospitality, handling up to 70% of queries autonomously and freeing human staff for trickier tasks.

Why This Project?

Customer support bots are a perfect entry point into AI agent development. They're practical—businesses use them daily to cut costs and boost satisfaction. They're also versatile, letting you explore key concepts like natural language processing, decision-making, and integration with external systems. Plus, they're scalable: start small with a local script, then grow it into a cloud-based system handling thousands of users. This project mirrors real-world demands, where companies like Amazon and Zendesk rely on similar bots, giving you a tangible outcome you can adapt for personal or professional use.

How It Evolves Across the Book

This bot isn't a one-chapter wonder—it grows with you, chapter by chapter, reflecting the skills you'll master:

- **Chapter 2: Setting Up the Development Environment**: You'll install Python and libraries like LangChain, laying the groundwork to code the bot.

- **Chapter 3: Understanding AI Agent Frameworks**: You'll pick LangChain as the framework, learning its components to shape the bot's structure.

- **Chapter 4: Building Basic AI Agents with LangChain**: Here, the bot takes its first form—a simple agent using the ReAct pattern to answer FAQs from a predefined list.

- **Chapter 5: Advanced Agent Development**: Add memory so it recalls past interactions (e.g., "You asked about shipping last time—here's an update") and handles more complex queries.

- **Chapter 6: Multi-Agent Systems**: Introduce a second agent to escalate issues—like refund requests—to, showing how agents collaborate.

- **Chapter 7: Integrating with External Services**: Connect the bot to a mock customer database or a live API (e.g., Slack), pulling real-time data like order status.

- **Chapter 8: Training and Optimizing AI Agents**: Train it to improve responses, using customer feedback to refine accuracy and tone.

- **Chapter 9: Testing and Debugging AI Agents**: Test it with edge cases (e.g., angry customers) and debug glitches to ensure reliability.

- **Chapter 10: Deploying AI Agents**: Deploy it on a cloud platform like AWS, making it available to handle multiple users simultaneously.

- **Chapter 11: Ethical Considerations**: Address bias in responses and privacy in handling customer data, ensuring it's fair and secure.

- **Chapter 12: Real-World Use Cases**: Compare it to industry bots, then tweak it for a specific niche, like tech support.

- **Chapter 13: Emerging Trends**: Upgrade it with 2025 trends, like multi-modal input (text and voice) or proactive suggestions (e.g., "Your warranty's expiring—renew now?").

Each step builds on the last, turning a basic script into a robust, real-world-ready agent.

Initial Requirements

Let's sketch out what this bot needs to start. It should:

- Understand and respond to basic customer questions using natural language.

- Access a knowledge base (e.g., a text file of FAQs) to provide accurate answers.

- Be user-friendly, with clear, concise replies.

- Run locally at first, with potential to scale later.

As it grows, it'll need memory to track conversations, integration with external systems, and the ability to collaborate or escalate. For now, think of it as a helpful assistant for a small online store—say, answering queries about shipping, returns, and product details.

Your Role and First Steps

You're the developer, and this project is your playground. At the end of this chapter, you'll find an exercise to brainstorm its initial features—questions it should answer, tone it should take (friendly? formal?), and any extra capabilities you'd like (e.g., multilingual support). This isn't just planning— it's your first step toward coding it in Chapter 4. Feel free to personalize it— maybe it's for a bookstore, a tech startup, or even a fictional business you dream up. The goal is to make it yours while learning the ropes.

Why It Matters in 2025

In 2025, customer support bots are everywhere, driving efficiency and customer satisfaction. Businesses report slashing response times and handling 70% of queries without human help, with some, like Salesforce, seeing 30% productivity boosts from AI agents. This project puts you in that game, teaching you skills that match industry needs—whether you're building for a job, a side project, or a startup. It's not just a bot; it's a portfolio piece showing you can tackle real-world AI challenges.

Building this customer support bot is your ticket to mastering AI agent development. It starts simple but grows into a powerful tool, reflecting the book's lessons in every line of code. By the end, you'll have a working agent that answers questions, learns from interactions, and scales to real users— all built with Python, the language powering 2025's AI revolution. Let's kick it off with that exercise and get ready to code something amazing.

Chapter 2: Setting Up the Development Environment

2.1 Installing Python and Necessary Libraries

Setting up your development environment is the first practical step toward building AI agents with Python. This section guides you through installing Python and a suite of essential libraries—LangChain, Hugging Face, CrewAI, Microsoft Semantic Kernel, AutoGen, LangGraph, BabyAGI, and Microsoft Copilot—that will power your projects, including the customer support bot introduced in Chapter 1. By the end of this process, you'll have a robust, ready-to-use setup tailored for AI agent development as of 2025. Whether you're on Windows, macOS, or Linux, these steps ensure you're equipped to code, test, and deploy agents efficiently.

Installing Python

Python is the foundation of this book, prized for its simplicity and vast AI ecosystem. As of 2025, Python 3.11 or 3.12 is recommended for its performance improvements and compatibility with modern libraries. Here's how to get it installed:

- **Step 1: Check Your System**: Open a terminal (Command Prompt on Windows, Terminal on macOS/Linux) and type python --version or python3 --version. If Python 3.11+ is already installed, you'll see the version number (e.g., **Python 3.12.1**). If not, proceed to download it.

- **Step 2: Download Python**: Visit the official Python website (**python.org**) and grab the latest stable release (e.g., 3.12). Choose the installer for your operating system—Windows executable, macOS package, or Linux source.

- **Step 3: Install Python**:

    - **Windows**: Run the installer, check "**Add Python to PATH**," and select "**Install Now.**" Verify with python --version in Command Prompt.

    - **macOS**: Open the .pkg file, follow the prompts, and confirm with python3 --version in Terminal.

- Linux: Use your package manager (e.g., sudo apt update && sudo apt install python3.12 on Ubuntu) or compile from source if needed, then check with python3 --version.

- **Step 4: Install pip**: Python's package manager, pip, should come bundled. Confirm with pip --version (or pip3 --version). If missing, download get-pip.py from python.org and run python get-pip.py.

With Python ready, you've got the base to layer on AI-specific tools.

Setting Up a Virtual Environment

Before installing libraries, create a virtual environment to keep your project dependencies isolated and manageable:

- **Step 1: Create It**: In your terminal, navigate to your project folder (e.g., cd my-ai-project) and run python -m *venv venv*. This creates a folder named **venv** for your environment.

- **Step 2: Activate It**:

  - **Windows: venv\Scripts\activate**

  - **macOS/Linux**: source venv/bin/activate You'll see **(venv)** in your prompt, signaling it's active.

- **Step 3: Verify**: Run python --version to ensure it's using the virtual environment's Python. Deactivate later with deactivate if needed.

This keeps your setup clean, avoiding conflicts between projects.

Installing Necessary Libraries

Now, install the libraries that will drive your AI agents. Each serves a unique role, and as of 2025, they're staples in the AI ecosystem. Use pip within your active virtual environment:

- **LangChain**: A framework for building context-aware agents with memory and tool integration.

  - Install: **pip install langchain**

- Purpose: Powers the customer support bot with natural language understanding and action-taking capabilities (e.g., answering FAQs in Chapter 4).

- Note: You might need pip install langchain-community for extra features like embeddings.

- **Hugging Face (Transformers)**: Provides pre-trained models for tasks like text generation and classification.

  - Install: **pip install transformers**

  - Purpose: Enhances your bot with advanced language models (e.g., fine-tuning responses in Chapter 8).

  - Extra: Add **pip install torch** for PyTorch support if GPU acceleration is desired.

- **CrewAI**: Facilitates multi-agent systems where agents collaborate on tasks.

  - Install: pip install crewai

  - Purpose: Enables the bot to escalate issues to a second agent (Chapter 6), simulating team workflows.

  - Tip: Check for updates, as CrewAI evolves rapidly in 2025.

- **Microsoft Semantic Kernel**: An enterprise-grade framework for integrating AI into applications.

  - Install: pip install semantic-kernel

  - Purpose: Offers robust tools for complex agent logic, useful for scaling the bot (Chapter 10).

  - Note: Requires .NET SDK for some features—skip if focusing on Python-only workflows.

- **AutoGen**: Automates agent creation and interaction, ideal for rapid prototyping.

  - Install: pip install pyautogen

- Purpose: Speeds up building agent prototypes (Chapter 3) and experimenting with designs.

- Extra: Ensure pip install requests for API interactions.

- **LangGraph**: Extends LangChain for graph-based agent workflows.

  - Install: pip install langgraph

  - Purpose: Structures the bot's decision-making as a graph (Chapter 5), enhancing complexity handling.

  - Tip: Pairs well with LangChain—install together for synergy.

- **BabyAGI**: A lightweight framework for task-driven agents inspired by AGI concepts.

  - Install: pip install babyagi (or clone from its GitHub if not on PyPI in 2025)

  - Purpose: Adds task prioritization to the bot (Chapter 5), mimicking human-like focus.

  - Note: May require manual setup—check the latest repo for instructions.

- **Microsoft Copilot (via GitHub Copilot SDK)**: AI-assisted coding support (not a traditional library but accessible via tools).

  - Setup: Install GitHub Copilot in your IDE (e.g., VS Code) with a subscription, or use open alternatives like pip install codeium if available.

  - Purpose: Boosts coding efficiency throughout the book, suggesting agent logic as you type.

  - Tip: Requires an IDE setup—configure before diving in.

Additional Dependencies

Some libraries need extras for full functionality:

- **NumPy and Pandas**: For data handling—pip install numpy pandas.

- **Requests**: For API calls—pip install requests.

- **Torch**: For GPU support with Hugging Face—pip install torch (check CUDA compatibility if using a GPU).

Run pip list to confirm all are installed. Update with pip install --upgrade <library> if versions lag.

Verifying the Setup

Test your environment:

- **Python**: Run python -c "import sys; print(sys.version)" to confirm the version.

- **Libraries**: Try python -c "import langchain, transformers, crewai" (add others as needed). No errors mean success.

- **Simple Test**: Write a quick script:

python

```
from langchain.llms import OpenAI

print("LangChain is ready!")
```
(Note: LangChain may require an API key—skip or configure one from openai.com for this test.)

If imports fail, re-run pip install or check for typos/version conflicts.

Troubleshooting Tips

- **Permission Errors**: Use pip install --user or run as admin (e.g., sudo on Linux).

- **Version Issues**: Specify versions (e.g., pip install langchain==0.1.0) if compatibility breaks.

- **Missing Dependencies**: Some libraries pull extras—install manually if prompted (e.g., pip install torch for Transformers).

- **OS-Specific Fixes**: Windows may need Visual Studio Build Tools for certain compiles; Linux might need python3-dev.

Why This Matters

This setup isn't just busywork—it's the foundation for every agent you'll build, including the customer support bot. LangChain drives its core logic, Hugging Face enhances its language skills, and CrewAI adds collaboration. By 2025, these tools are industry standards, powering bots that handle 70% of customer queries or optimize workflows with 30% productivity gains. Getting them installed now means you're ready to code, experiment, and deploy with confidence.

Exercise Prep

At chapter's end, you'll verify this setup with an exercise—running a script to ensure all libraries work. It's your first taste of agent-building, setting the stage for Chapter 4's hands-on coding. For now, install, test, and get comfortable—this is where your AI journey begins.

Installing Python and these libraries equips you with a powerhouse environment for AI agent development. Each tool brings something unique—LangChain's flexibility, Hugging Face's models, CrewAI's teamwork—readying you for the customer support bot and beyond. With this done, you're not just set up; you're poised to create agents that solve real problems in 2025's AI-driven world. Let's get coding.

2.2 Configuring API Keys and Environment Variables

Once Python and your core libraries are installed, the next step in setting up your development environment is configuring API keys and environment variables. Many AI agent libraries—like LangChain, Hugging Face, and AutoGen—rely on external services, such as large language models or cloud platforms, which require secure authentication via API keys. Environment variables keep these keys safe, organized, and out of your codebase, ensuring your projects, including the customer support bot, run smoothly and securely. This section walks you through obtaining keys, setting them up, and testing them as of 2025, so you're ready to power your agents with cutting-edge AI services.

Why API Keys and Environment Variables Matter

API keys are unique codes that authenticate your access to third-party services, like OpenAI's language models or AWS cloud resources. Hardcoding them in your scripts is risky—think accidental leaks in version control or cluttered code. Environment variables solve this by storing sensitive data outside your scripts, accessible only when needed. This practice is industry-standard in 2025, aligning with security best practices and making your code portable across machines or deployments (e.g., from local testing to cloud hosting for the bot).

Step 1: Obtaining API Keys

You'll need keys for the services powering your libraries. Here's how to get them for the main ones:

- **OpenAI (for LangChain and General LLMs)**:
    - Sign up at openai.com, log in, and navigate to the API section.
    - Generate a key (e.g., sk-abc123...) under "API Keys." Copy it—you won't see it again.
    - Cost: Free tier offers limited credits; plans start at $5/month in 2025 for heavier use.

- **Hugging Face (for Transformers)**:
    - Register at huggingface.co, go to your profile, and select **"Access Tokens."**
    - Create a token (e.g., hf_xyz789...) with read/write permissions. Save it securely.
    - Cost: Free for most models; premium models may require a subscription ($9/month+).

- **AWS (for Deployment in Chapter 10)**:

- Sign into aws.amazon.com, go to "IAM" (Identity and Access Management), and create a user.

- Assign permissions (e.g., Lambda, S3), then generate an access key pair (Access Key ID and Secret Access Key, like AKIA... and abcd...).

- Cost: Free to create; usage fees apply later (e.g., $0.02/hour for Lambda).

- **Others (CrewAI, AutoGen, etc.)**:

  - Check each library's docs in 2025—CrewAI might use custom APIs, AutoGen may leverage OpenAI or others. Visit their official sites (e.g., crewai.com, autogen.ai) for key generation steps.

  - Example: If CrewAI integrates with a service like Anthropic, sign up there for a key (e.g., anthropic-123...).

Keep these keys in a secure place (e.g., a password manager)—you'll need them shortly.

Step 2: Setting Up Environment Variables

With keys in hand, store them as environment variables so your Python scripts can access them without hardcoding. The process varies by operating system:

- **Windows**:

  1. Open Command Prompt as admin.

  2. Set a variable with: setx OPENAI_API_KEY "sk-abc123..." (replace with your key). Repeat for others (e.g., setx HUGGINGFACE_TOKEN "hf_xyz789...").

  3. Close and reopen Command Prompt to apply. Check with echo %OPENAI_API_KEY%.

- **macOS/Linux**:

  1. Open Terminal and edit your shell config file:

- Bash: nano ~/.bashrc or nano ~/.bash_profile

- Zsh (common in 2025): nano ~/.zshrc

2. Add lines like:

3. export OPENAI_API_KEY="sk-abc123..."

4. export HUGGINGFACE_TOKEN="hf_xyz789..."

5. export AWS_ACCESS_KEY_ID="AKIA..."

export AWS_SECRET_ACCESS_KEY="abcd..."

6. Save (Ctrl+O, Enter, Ctrl+X in nano), then run source ~/.bashrc (or .zshrc) to apply. Verify with echo $OPENAI_API_KEY.

- **Virtual Environment Option**:

  o For project-specific keys, use a .env file in your project folder (e.g., my-ai-project/):

  o OPENAI_API_KEY=sk-abc123...

  o HUGGINGFACE_TOKEN=hf_xyz789...

  o AWS_ACCESS_KEY_ID=AKIA...

AWS_SECRET_ACCESS_KEY=abcd...

  o Install python-dotenv: pip install python-dotenv.

  o Load in Python (see Step 3).

This keeps keys local to your project, ideal for the customer support bot.

Step 3: Accessing Keys in Python

Your scripts need to retrieve these variables securely. Here's how:

- **Direct Access** (System Variables):

python

```
import os
```

```python
openai_key = os.getenv("OPENAI_API_KEY")

huggingface_token = os.getenv("HUGGINGFACE_TOKEN")

print("OpenAI Key:", openai_key)  # Test it
```

- **Using** .env **File**:

python

```python
from dotenv import load_dotenv

import os

load_dotenv()  # Loads from .env in project root

openai_key = os.getenv("OPENAI_API_KEY")

huggingface_token = os.getenv("HUGGINGFACE_TOKEN")

print("OpenAI Key:", openai_key)
```

Add this to your scripts' start. If None prints, check your variable setup.

Step 4: Configuring Libraries with Keys

Each library uses keys differently—here's how to set them up:

- **LangChain**:

python

```python
from langchain.llms import OpenAI

llm = OpenAI(api_key=os.getenv("OPENAI_API_KEY"))

print(llm("Hello, world!"))  # Test call
```

- Needs an OpenAI key; errors if unset.

- **Hugging Face**:

python

```python
from transformers import pipeline

generator = pipeline("text-generation", model="gpt2",
token=os.getenv("HUGGINGFACE_TOKEN"))
```

```python
print(generator("Hi there")[0]["generated_text"])
```

- Token optional for free models, required for premium.

- **AWS (for Later)**:

```python
import boto3

session = boto3.Session(
    aws_access_key_id=os.getenv("AWS_ACCESS_KEY_ID"),
    aws_secret_access_key=os.getenv("AWS_SECRET_ACCESS_KEY")
)
```

- Used in Chapter 10 for deployment.

- **CrewAI/AutoGen**: Check their 2025 docs—often use OpenAI keys or custom ones:

```python
# Example for CrewAI (hypothetical)
from crewai import Agent

agent = Agent(api_key=os.getenv("CREWAI_API_KEY"))
```

Step 5: Testing the Configuration

Verify everything works:

- Run a script combining LangChain and Hugging Face:

```python
from dotenv import load_dotenv

import os

from langchain.llms import OpenAI

load_dotenv()

llm = OpenAI(api_key=os.getenv("OPENAI_API_KEY"))
```

```
print(llm("Test my setup"))
```
- Expect a response like "Your setup is working!" If not, check keys, variables, or internet connection.

Security Best Practices

- **Never Commit Keys**: Add .env to .gitignore if using Git.

- **Limit Key Scope**: Use least-privilege keys (e.g., read-only for Hugging Face unless writing).

- **Rotate Keys**: Update periodically via service dashboards, then refresh environment variables.

Why This Matters for the Bot

The customer support bot relies on these APIs—LangChain needs OpenAI for language processing, Hugging Face for model enhancements, and AWS for deployment. Configuring keys now ensures it can answer FAQs in Chapter 4, integrate with services in Chapter 7, and scale in Chapter 10. In 2025, secure API use is non-negotiable, with bots handling sensitive customer data safely.

Exercise Prep

Chapter 2's exercise will test these keys with a simple agent call, confirming your setup. It's your first real interaction with the bot's foundation—get this right, and you're set for coding.

Configuring API keys and environment variables locks in your ability to tap powerful AI services securely. With OpenAI, Hugging Face, and others at your fingertips, you're ready to build the customer support bot and beyond. This setup is your bridge from local code to real-world impact—let's make it work.

2.3 Setting Up a Virtual Environment

A virtual environment is a critical tool for AI agent development, creating an isolated space where you can install Python and its libraries—like LangChain, Hugging Face, and CrewAI—without cluttering or conflicting with your system's global setup. This section walks you through setting up a virtual environment for your projects, including the customer support bot, ensuring a clean, reproducible workspace as of 2025. By keeping dependencies separate, you'll avoid version mismatches and make your code portable, whether you're testing locally or preparing for cloud deployment. Let's get it done step-by-step.

Why Use a Virtual Environment?

Think of a virtual environment as a sandbox for your project. Without it, installing libraries globally could overwrite versions needed by other programs—like LangChain 0.1.0 clashing with 0.2.0—or create a mess of dependencies. For the customer support bot, you'll use specific library versions (e.g., LangChain for its ReAct pattern, Hugging Face for models), and a virtual environment keeps these isolated. It's also a 2025 best practice: it mimics production setups, simplifies collaboration (just share the environment specs), and prevents "it works on my machine" headaches. Plus, it's lightweight—no extra software, just Python's built-in tools.

Step 1: Ensure Python Is Installed

You need Python 3.11 or 3.12 installed (see Section 2.1). Verify with:

- Terminal: python --version (Windows) or python3 --version (macOS/Linux).

- Output should show, e.g., "Python 3.12.1." If not, revisit Section 2.1 to install.

Step 2: Create the Virtual Environment

With Python ready, create your environment:

- **Choose a Project Folder**: Pick or make a directory for your work, like my-ai-project. Navigate there:
    - Windows (Command Prompt): cd C:\path\to\my-ai-project
    - macOS/Linux (Terminal): cd ~/path/to/my-ai-project
- **Run the Command**: Use Python's venv module:
    - python -m venv venv

- o This creates a folder named venv (you can name it anything, but venv is standard) containing a fresh Python setup.
- **What Happens**: Inside venv, you'll find:
  - o bin (or Scripts on Windows): Python executables and scripts.
  - o lib: Library storage for your installs.
  - o A copy of your system's Python, isolated from the global one.

Step 3: Activate the Virtual Environment

Activating switches your terminal to use this isolated setup:

- **Windows**:
  - o venv\Scripts\activate
  - o Prompt changes to (venv) C:\path\to\my-ai-project>.
- **macOS/Linux**:
  - o source venv/bin/activate
  - o Prompt becomes (venv) user@machine:~/path/to/my-ai-project$.
- **Verify**: Run python --version—it should match your system Python but now runs from venv. Check pip --version too—it'll point to venv's pip (e.g., pip 23.3 from .../venv/...).

If (venv) doesn't appear, double-check the path or command syntax.

Step 4: Install Libraries Inside the Environment

With the environment active, install your AI agent libraries (detailed in Section 2.1):

- pip install langchain transformers crewai semantic-kernel pyautogen langgraph babyagi
- Add extras: pip install numpy pandas requests python-dotenv (for data, APIs, and .env files).

- Optional (for Hugging Face GPU): pip install torch (check your GPU's CUDA version if applicable).

- Confirm: pip list shows installed packages (e.g., langchain 0.1.0, transformers 4.35.0).

These stay local to venv, leaving your system Python untouched.

Step 5: Deactivating the Environment

When done, exit the sandbox:

- deactivate

- Prompt returns to normal (e.g., C:\path\to\my-ai-project> or user@machine:~/path/to$).

- Reactivate anytime with the activation command—your libraries persist in venv.

Step 6: Managing Multiple Environments

For different projects—like tweaking the bot for tech support vs. e-commerce—create separate environments:

- In a new folder (e.g., bot-v2): python -m venv venv

- Activate and install as needed. Name them uniquely (e.g., bot1_env, bot2_env) to avoid confusion.

Sharing Your Setup

To collaborate or replicate your environment:

- **Export Requirements**: Run pip freeze > requirements.txt while active. This lists all installed packages and versions (e.g., langchain==0.1.0).

- **Share**: Send requirements.txt with your code.

- **Recreate**: Others (or you on a new machine) activate a fresh venv, then run pip install -r requirements.txt to match your setup exactly.

This ensures the customer support bot runs consistently everywhere.

Troubleshooting

- **Command Not Found**: Use python3 instead of python on macOS/Linux if python isn't linked (e.g., python3 -m venv venv).

- **Permission Errors**: Avoid system folders—use a user directory (e.g., C:\Users\You\Projects).

- **Activation Fails**: Check the path to venv—typos like ven\Scripts\activate (missing v) break it.

- **Old Versions**: Upgrade pip inside venv with pip install --upgrade pip if installs fail.

Why This Matters for the Bot

The customer support bot needs a tailored environment—LangChain for its core, Hugging Face for language models, CrewAI for multi-agent features—all version-specific to work together. A virtual environment ensures these play nice, avoiding conflicts with, say, a global Python setup for web dev. In 2025, with bots handling 70% of queries or boosting productivity by 30%, a clean setup is your launchpad to replicate that success.

Exercise Prep

Chapter 2's exercise will have you activate this environment, install libraries, and test a basic script—your first step toward the bot in Chapter 4. Get this right, and you're locked in for hands-on coding.

Setting up a virtual environment is your ticket to a clean, controlled workspace for AI agent development. It's simple, keeps your bot's dependencies in check, and sets you up for success as you build, test, and deploy with Python in 2025. With venv active, you're ready to load it with tools and start crafting agents that matter—let's keep the momentum going.

2.4 Exercise: Set Up Your Development Environment and Verify Installation

Now it's time to roll up your sleeves and put the pieces together. This exercise guides you through setting up your complete development environment—installing Python, creating a virtual environment, adding essential AI libraries, and configuring API keys—then verifying everything works with a simple test script. By the end, you'll have a fully functional setup ready to build the customer support bot and beyond, tailored for 2025's AI agent development landscape. This hands-on task ensures you're not just reading about it but doing it, locking in the skills from Sections 2.1 to 2.3.

Objectives

- Install Python 3.12 and confirm it's running.

- Set up a virtual environment to isolate your project.

- Install key libraries: LangChain, Hugging Face, CrewAI, Microsoft Semantic Kernel, AutoGen, LangGraph, BabyAGI, and extras.

- Configure API keys for OpenAI and Hugging Face using environment variables.

- Run a test script to verify the setup, ensuring all components are operational.

Step-by-Step Instructions

Part 1: Install Python

1. **Check Existing Version**:

   o Open a terminal (Command Prompt on Windows, Terminal on macOS/Linux).

   o Run python --version (Windows) or python3 --version (macOS/Linux).

   o If it's 3.11 or 3.12 (e.g., "Python 3.12.1"), skip to Part 2. If not, proceed.

2. **Download and Install**:

   o Go to python.org, download Python 3.12 for your OS (Windows .exe, macOS .pkg, Linux source).

- Windows: Run the installer, check "Add Python to PATH," click "Install Now."

- macOS: Open the .pkg, follow prompts.

- Linux: Use sudo apt update && sudo apt install python3.12 (Ubuntu) or equivalent.

3. **Verify**:

- Run python --version (or python3 --version). Expect "Python 3.12.x."

- Confirm pip: pip --version (or pip3 --version). If missing, run python -m ensurepip --upgrade then python -m pip install --upgrade pip.

Part 2: Set Up a Virtual Environment

1. **Create a Project Folder**:

- Make a directory, e.g., mkdir ai-agent-dev and cd ai-agent-dev.

2. **Create the Environment**:

- Run python -m venv venv (or python3 -m venv venv on macOS/Linux).

- A venv folder appears in your directory.

3. **Activate It**:

- **Windows**: venv\Scripts\activate

- **macOS/Linux**: source venv/bin/activate

- See (venv) in your prompt.

4. **Verify**:

- Run python --version—should match your installed version, now from venv.

- Check pip --version—points to venv's pip.

Part 3: Install Libraries

1. **Core AI Libraries** (with (venv) active):

    o   Run:

pip install langchain transformers crewai semantic-kernel pyautogen
langgraph babyagi

    o   Notes:

        ▪   transformers is Hugging Face's library.

        ▪   semantic-kernel is Microsoft Semantic Kernel.

        ▪   pyautogen is AutoGen.

        ▪   If babyagi fails, skip for now—it may need GitHub
            cloning in 2025.

2. **Extras**:

    o   pip install numpy pandas requests python-dotenv

    o   Optional (GPU): pip install torch (check CUDA compatibility if
        using a GPU).

3. **Verify**:

    o   Run pip list—look for installed packages (e.g., langchain,
        transformers).

Part 4: Configure API Keys

1. **Obtain Keys**:

    o   **OpenAI**: Sign up at openai.com, go to API section, generate a
        key (e.g., sk-abc123...).

    o   **Hugging Face**: Register at huggingface.co, create a token in
        "Access Tokens" (e.g., hf_xyz789...).

2. **Set Environment Variables**:

    o   Create a .env file in ai-agent-dev:

- o   OPENAI_API_KEY=sk-abc123...

HUGGINGFACE_TOKEN=hf_xyz789...

- o   Save it (use a text editor like Notepad or nano).

3. **Test Access**:

- o   Run python -c "import os;
    print(os.getenv('OPENAI_API_KEY'))"—should print None
    (not loaded yet).

Part 5: Verify with a Test Script

1. **Write the Script**:

- o   In ai-agent-dev, create test_setup.py:

python

```
from dotenv import load_dotenv

import os

from langchain.llms import OpenAI

from transformers import pipeline


# Load environment variables

load_dotenv()


# Check API keys

openai_key = os.getenv("OPENAI_API_KEY")

hf_token = os.getenv("HUGGINGFACE_TOKEN")

print(f"OpenAI Key Loaded: {'Yes' if openai_key else 'No'}")
```

```python
print(f"Hugging Face Token Loaded: {'Yes' if hf_token else 'No'}")


# Test LangChain with OpenAI
if openai_key:
    llm = OpenAI(api_key=openai_key)
    response = llm("Hello, is my setup working?")
    print("LangChain Response:", response)
else:
    print("Skipping LangChain test—no OpenAI key.")


# Test Hugging Face
generator = pipeline("text-generation", model="gpt2", token=hf_token)
output = generator("Testing my setup", max_length=20)[0]["generated_text"]
print("Hugging Face Response:", output)


# Confirm other imports
import crewai, semantic_kernel, pyautogen, langgraph
print("All libraries imported successfully!")
```

2. **Run It**:

    o   python test_setup.py

    o   Expected Output (example):

- o OpenAI Key Loaded: Yes

- o Hugging Face Token Loaded: Yes

- o LangChain Response: Yes, your setup is working great!

- o Hugging Face Response: Testing my setup is working fine

All libraries imported successfully!

- o If BabyAGI is missing, you'll see an import error—safe to ignore for now.

Troubleshooting

- **Python Not Found**: Use python3 on macOS/Linux or fix PATH (reinstall with "Add to PATH").

- **Pip Fails**: Upgrade with python -m pip install --upgrade pip.

- **Import Errors**: Re-run pip install <library> or check spelling (e.g., pyautogen not autogen).

- **API Key Errors**: Ensure .env is in the right folder, no typos, and load_dotenv() is called.

- **No Response**: Check internet (API calls need it) or key validity (regenerate if expired).

What Success Looks Like

- Python runs, (venv) is active, and libraries install without errors.

- The script prints responses from LangChain and Hugging Face, confirming API keys and imports work.

- You're ready for Chapter 4's bot-coding with a solid foundation.

Why This Matters

This setup powers the customer support bot—LangChain for its logic, Hugging Face for language, and more—all in a clean environment. In 2025, a working setup like this is your gateway to building agents that handle 70% of queries or boost productivity by 30%, mirroring industry standards. This exercise proves you're not just set up but operational.

You've built your AI agent workbench—Python, libraries, keys, and all—verified with a script that ties it together. This isn't just prep; it's your first win in mastering AI development. With this environment humming, you're primed to code the customer support bot and tackle any agent project in 2025. Great job—let's keep building!

Chapter 3: Understanding AI Agent Frameworks

3.1 Overview of Popular Frameworks

AI agent frameworks are the engines that simplify building intelligent, autonomous systems, and as of 2025, they're essential for crafting everything from chatbots to multi-agent teams. This section introduces you to the leading frameworks—LangChain, CrewAI, Microsoft Semantic Kernel, AutoGen, LangGraph, BabyAGI, and Microsoft Copilot—each offering unique strengths for developing AI agents like the customer support bot you'll build. By understanding their purposes, components, and use cases, you'll gain the insight to choose the right tool for your project, whether it's a simple FAQ bot or a complex, collaborative system. Let's dive into what makes these frameworks tick and why they matter.

Why Frameworks Matter

Building an AI agent from scratch—coding perception, reasoning, and actions—is like reinventing the wheel. Frameworks provide pre-built structures, integrating AI techniques like language models, memory, and tool use, so you can focus on designing behavior rather than wrestling with low-level details. In 2025, they're the backbone of agent development, powering solutions that handle 70% of customer queries or boost productivity by 30%. Each framework here is Python-friendly, aligning with this book's focus, and offers a mix of flexibility, power, and ease to suit different needs.

LangChain

- **What It Is**: LangChain is a versatile framework for building context-aware AI agents that leverage large language models (LLMs) with memory and external tools.

- **Key Features**:
    - Integrates LLMs (e.g., OpenAI, Hugging Face models) for natural language processing.

- Adds memory (short-term and long-term) so agents remember past interactions.

- Supports tools—APIs, databases, web scraping—for real-world actions.

- Uses patterns like ReAct (Reasoning + Acting) for decision-making.

- **Use Case**: Perfect for the customer support bot—answering FAQs with a knowledge base (Chapter 4), remembering chats (Chapter 5), and integrating with APIs (Chapter 7).

- **Strengths**: Easy to start, highly customizable, and widely adopted in 2025 for single-agent tasks.

- **Setup**: pip install langchain—pairs with OpenAI keys or local models.

CrewAI

- **What It Is**: CrewAI specializes in multi-agent systems, enabling teams of agents to collaborate on complex tasks with defined roles.

- **Key Features**:

  - Assigns roles (e.g., researcher, writer) and goals to individual agents.

  - Manages communication and task handoffs between agents.

  - Integrates with LLMs and tools for execution.

- **Use Case**: Ideal for enhancing the bot in Chapter 6—adding a second agent to escalate refund requests while the main bot handles queries.

- **Strengths**: Simplifies multi-agent coordination, scalable for teamwork scenarios like logistics or content creation.

- **Setup**: pip install crewai—often uses OpenAI or similar LLMs.

Microsoft Semantic Kernel

- **What It Is**: An enterprise-grade framework for integrating AI into applications, blending LLMs with structured workflows and memory.

- **Key Features**:

  - Combines "skills" (pre-built functions) with LLM reasoning.

  - Offers memory management for context retention.

  - Supports connectors to enterprise systems (e.g., Microsoft 365, Azure).

- **Use Case**: Suits scaling the bot in Chapter 10—deploying it with enterprise-grade reliability and connecting to business tools.

- **Strengths**: Robust for professional settings, strong Microsoft ecosystem integration, but steeper learning curve.

- **Setup**: pip install semantic-kernel—best with Azure or Microsoft services.

AutoGen

- **What It Is**: AutoGen automates agent creation and interaction, emphasizing rapid prototyping and human-in-the-loop workflows.

- **Key Features**:

  - Generates agents from high-level specs (e.g., "build a chatbot").

  - Supports multi-agent conversations with humans moderating.

  - Integrates LLMs and tools with minimal code.

- **Use Case**: Great for quick prototypes in Chapter 3 or experimenting with bot variations before refining in later chapters.

- **Strengths**: Fast setup, flexible for testing ideas, good for collaborative agent-human systems.

- **Setup**: pip install pyautogen—relies on OpenAI or similar APIs.

LangGraph

- **What It Is**: An extension of LangChain, LangGraph structures agent workflows as graphs, ideal for complex, stateful interactions.

- **Key Features**:

  - Models agent logic as nodes (actions) and edges (transitions).

  - Handles memory and branching decisions (e.g., if-then logic).

  - Integrates with LangChain's LLMs and tools.

- **Use Case**: Enhances the bot in Chapter 5—structuring its decision-making (e.g., "if query is complex, escalate") as a graph.

- **Strengths**: Precise control over workflows, perfect for intricate single agents, builds on LangChain familiarity.

- **Setup**: pip install langgraph—works best with LangChain installed.

BabyAGI

- **What It Is**: BabyAGI is a lightweight, task-driven framework inspired by artificial general intelligence (AGI), focusing on goal-oriented agents.

- **Key Features**:

  - Breaks goals into tasks, prioritizes them, and iterates execution.

  - Uses LLMs for reasoning and task generation.

  - Simple, minimal codebase for experimentation.

- **Use Case**: Useful in Chapter 5 for adding task prioritization to the bot—like handling urgent queries first.

- **Strengths**: Lean and flexible, great for learning agent fundamentals, but less polished than others.

- **Setup**: pip install babyagi (or clone from GitHub if not on PyPI in 2025)—needs manual tweaking.

Microsoft Copilot

- **What It Is**: Microsoft Copilot isn't a traditional framework but an AI-assisted coding tool integrated into IDEs like VS Code, enhancing development.

- **Key Features**:

    - Suggests code, completes agent logic, and explains snippets.

    - Works with Python and your chosen frameworks.

    - Powered by LLMs, trainable on your codebase.

- **Use Case**: Boosts productivity across all chapters—e.g., suggesting ReAct code in Chapter 4 or deployment scripts in Chapter 10.

- **Strengths**: Seamless coding aid, reduces boilerplate, but requires a subscription and IDE setup.

- **Setup**: Install via VS Code marketplace with a GitHub Copilot account—alternatives like Codeium may be free.

Comparing the Frameworks

Here's a quick rundown to help you choose:

- **Ease of Use**: LangChain and AutoGen win for quick starts; Semantic Kernel and CrewAI need more setup.

- **Single vs. Multi-Agent**: LangChain, LangGraph, and BabyAGI excel for single agents; CrewAI and AutoGen shine for multi-agent.

- **Enterprise Focus**: Semantic Kernel leads for business integration; others are more general-purpose.

- **Complexity**: BabyAGI is simplest; LangGraph and Semantic Kernel offer advanced control.

- **Coding Support**: Copilot aids all frameworks, not a builder itself.

For the customer support bot, LangChain is the primary pick—its versatility covers Chapters 4-7—while CrewAI adds multi-agent flair in Chapter 6, and LangGraph refines logic in Chapter 5.

Why This Matters for the Bot

The bot starts with LangChain in Chapter 4, answering FAQs with ReAct. CrewAI joins in Chapter 6 for escalation, and LangGraph could structure its flow in Chapter 5. Copilot speeds up coding throughout. In 2025, these frameworks power real-world bots handling 70% of queries—understanding them here sets you up to replicate that success.

Next Steps

Chapter 3 digs deeper into framework components (Section 3.2) and picking one (Section 3.3). This overview primes you to explore and experiment, starting with a LangChain-based bot in Chapter 4.

LangChain, CrewAI, Semantic Kernel, AutoGen, LangGraph, BabyAGI, and Copilot form a powerhouse lineup for AI agent development in 2025. Each brings something unique—whether it's LangChain's flexibility, CrewAI's teamwork, or Copilot's coding boost—giving you tools to build the customer support bot and beyond. With this foundation, you're ready to harness their strengths and craft agents that solve real problems. Let's keep going.

3.2 Key Components: LLMs, Prompts, Chains, Agents, Tools

Building AI agents isn't magic—it's assembling a set of core components that work together to perceive, reason, and act. Frameworks like LangChain, CrewAI, and AutoGen rely on five key pieces: Large Language Models (LLMs), prompts, chains, agents, and tools. These are the building blocks you'll use to create the customer support bot and other intelligent systems throughout this book. As of 2025, understanding how they fit together is essential for crafting agents that handle real-world tasks—like answering queries or escalating issues—with precision and adaptability. Let's break them down and see how they power your projects.

Large Language Models (LLMs)

- **What They Are**: LLMs are the brains behind AI agents, massive neural networks trained on vast text datasets to understand and generate human-like language. Examples include OpenAI's GPT-4,

Hugging Face's open-source models (e.g., LLaMA), or Anthropic's Claude.

- **Role**: They process inputs (e.g., "What's your return policy?") and produce outputs (e.g., "You can return items within 30 days."), enabling natural conversation and reasoning.

- **How They Work**: Trained on billions of words, they predict the next word or phrase based on context, fine-tuned for tasks like answering questions or summarizing text.

- **In the Bot**: The bot uses an LLM via LangChain to interpret customer queries and generate responses in Chapter 4, with Hugging Face models potentially enhancing it in Chapter 8.

- **Key Detail**: In 2025, LLMs are multi-modal—some handle text, images, and audio—boosting versatility (explored in Chapter 13).

Prompts

- **What They Are**: Prompts are instructions or questions you feed the LLM to guide its behavior, like a script for an actor. Think "Answer as a friendly support agent" or "Summarize this FAQ."

- **Role**: They shape the LLM's output—without a good prompt, responses can be vague or off-topic. A well-crafted prompt ensures the bot stays on task.

- **How They Work**: Written in natural language, they set the tone, context, and goal. For example, "You're a customer support bot for a bookstore. Respond concisely" keeps answers relevant.

- **In the Bot**: In Chapter 4, you'll craft a prompt like "Use this FAQ list to answer user questions accurately" to kick off the bot's basic functionality.

- **Key Detail**: Prompts evolved by 2025—dynamic prompts adjust based on context (e.g., prior chats), a trick you'll refine in Chapter 5.

Chains

- **What They Are**: Chains are sequences of steps combining LLMs, prompts, and data to process complex tasks—like a recipe linking ingredients and instructions.

- **Role**: They break down big jobs into manageable parts. A chain might take a query, fetch an answer from a database, and format it with an LLM.

- **How They Work**: In LangChain, a chain could be: 1) Prompt the LLM with "Extract key info from this text," 2) Pass the result to "Rephrase as a support answer." Output flows from one step to the next.

- **In the Bot**: By Chapter 5, a chain retrieves past chat history, feeds it to the LLM with a prompt, and generates a contextual reply (e.g., "Last time you asked about shipping—here's more info").

- **Key Detail**: Chains can loop or branch, adding logic like "if no answer found, search online," boosting flexibility.

Agents

- **What They Are**: Agents are the decision-makers, using LLMs, prompts, and chains to act autonomously—like the bot itself, not just its brain.

- **Role**: They decide *what* to do and *how*, combining reasoning with action. An agent might choose to answer a query, fetch data, or escalate to another agent.

- **How They Work**: Frameworks like LangChain use patterns like ReAct—reason (think through the query), act (respond or fetch info)—looping until the task's done. CrewAI assigns roles to agents for teamwork.

- **In the Bot**: The bot starts as a basic agent in Chapter 4 (ReAct: reason about the query, act with an FAQ answer), growing into a multi-agent system in Chapter 6 (e.g., escalating refunds).

- **Key Detail**: In 2025, agents are proactive—anticipating needs (Chapter 13)—not just reactive, a leap from earlier AI.

Tools

- **What They Are**: Tools are external capabilities agents use to interact with the world—APIs, databases, web scrapers, or even calculators.

- **Role**: They extend the LLM's reach beyond language. An LLM can't check order status alone, but a tool-connected agent can query a database and reply.

- **How They Work**: Frameworks integrate tools via APIs or functions. LangChain, for instance, lets an agent call a weather API or search Google if stumped.

- **In the Bot**: In Chapter 7, the bot uses a tool to pull order details from a mock API, replying "Your order #123 shipped today" instead of a generic answer.

- **Key Detail**: Tools are modular—add a new one (e.g., Slack integration), and the agent adapts without rewriting its core.

How They Fit Together

Picture the customer support bot:

- **LLM**: Understands "Where's my package?" (e.g., GPT-4 via LangChain).

- **Prompt**: "Answer as a support bot using this tracking data" keeps it focused.

- **Chain**: Steps: 1) Parse query, 2) Call tracking tool, 3) Format response ("It's in transit").

- **Agent**: Decides to use the chain or say "I don't know" if no data exists.

- **Tool**: Queries the shipping API for real-time status.

In Chapter 4, you'll start with an LLM, prompt, and agent for basic FAQs. By Chapter 5, chains add memory, and Chapter 7 brings tools—each component layering onto the last.

Why This Matters in 2025

These components are the DNA of modern agents—handling 70% of queries autonomously or boosting productivity by 30% in firms like Salesforce. LLMs provide smarts, prompts steer them, chains structure tasks, agents orchestrate, and tools connect to reality. For the bot, they're the difference between a static script and a dynamic helper, setting you up for real-world impact.

Next Steps

Section 3.3 helps you pick a framework to wield these components—LangChain for the bot's start, with others layering in later. Chapter 4 puts them into action with your first agent.

LLMs, prompts, chains, agents, and tools are the gears of AI agent frameworks, turning raw AI into practical solutions. Mastering them means mastering agents—whether it's the bot answering "Yes, we ship internationally" or escalating a refund. As you build with Python in 2025, these pieces will be your toolkit—let's start assembling them.

3.3 Comparing Different Frameworks

Choosing the right framework for your AI agent project—like the customer support bot—is a pivotal decision that shapes how efficiently and effectively you can build, scale, and deploy it. In Section 3.1, we introduced LangChain, CrewAI, Microsoft Semantic Kernel, AutoGen, LangGraph, BabyAGI, and Microsoft Copilot, each with unique strengths as of 2025. Now, we'll compare them across key dimensions—ease of use, scalability, multi-agent support, enterprise readiness, learning curve, and use case fit— to help you pick the best tool for the job. This analysis ensures you're equipped to start coding in Chapter 4 with confidence, leveraging the right framework for your goals.

Comparison Criteria

To evaluate these frameworks fairly, we'll use:

- **Ease of Use**: How quickly can you get started?

- **Scalability**: Can it grow from prototype to production?

- **Multi-Agent Support**: Does it handle agent collaboration?

- **Enterprise Readiness**: Is it suited for professional, large-scale use?

- **Learning Curve**: How much effort to master it?

- **Use Case Fit**: How well does it match the bot and other projects?

LangChain

- **Ease of Use**: High—intuitive API, quick setup with pip install langchain, and simple LLM integration (e.g., OpenAI in minutes).

- **Scalability**: Strong—handles single agents well, scales with tools and memory, but less optimized for massive multi-agent systems.

- **Multi-Agent Support**: Limited—focuses on single agents; multi-agent requires custom work or pairing with CrewAI.

- **Enterprise Readiness**: Moderate—flexible for small to mid-scale apps, but lacks built-in enterprise connectors (e.g., Azure).

- **Learning Curve**: Low—familiar to Python devs, with clear docs and examples like ReAct.

- **Use Case Fit**: Ideal for the bot's start in Chapter 4—FAQ answers with memory (Chapter 5) and tools (Chapter 7)—thanks to its versatility and simplicity.

- **Verdict**: Your go-to for the bot's foundation—easy, powerful, and grows with the project.

CrewAI

- **Ease of Use**: Moderate—requires defining roles and goals, but pip install crewai and examples ease the start.

- **Scalability**: High—designed for multi-agent teams, scales well for collaborative tasks across many agents.

- **Multi-Agent Support**: Excellent—its core strength, with built-in coordination (e.g., agent handoffs).

- **Enterprise Readiness**: Moderate—good for team workflows, but less focus on enterprise integrations.

- **Learning Curve**: Medium—multi-agent concepts add complexity, though Python syntax keeps it accessible.

- **Use Case Fit**: Perfect for Chapter 6's multi-agent bot—adding an escalation agent—where teamwork shines (e.g., support + refund agents).

- **Verdict**: Best for multi-agent scenarios, a natural add-on to LangChain later in the book.

Microsoft Semantic Kernel

- **Ease of Use**: Low—setup with pip install semantic-kernel is straightforward, but enterprise focus adds initial overhead.

- **Scalability**: Very High—built for large-scale apps, scales seamlessly with cloud and enterprise systems.

- **Multi-Agent Support**: Moderate—supports multiple skills, but multi-agent isn't its core; requires custom orchestration.

- **Enterprise Readiness**: Excellent—ties into Microsoft ecosystems (Azure, 365), ideal for professional deployments (Chapter 10).

- **Learning Curve**: High—steep for non-enterprise devs due to "skills" and connectors, plus optional .NET knowledge.

- **Use Case Fit**: Overkill for the bot's early stages, but great for Chapter 10's cloud deployment with enterprise-grade reliability.

- **Verdict**: A heavy hitter for scaling and enterprise—use it when the bot goes big.

AutoGen

- **Ease of Use**: High—pip install pyautogen and high-level specs (e.g., "build a chatbot") make prototyping fast.

- **Scalability**: Moderate—great for quick builds, less optimized for large, persistent systems without tweaks.

- **Multi-Agent Support**: Strong—excels at multi-agent conversations, especially with human-in-the-loop moderation.

- **Enterprise Readiness**: Low—focuses on flexibility over enterprise integrations, better for experimentation.

- **Learning Curve**: Low—simple for basic use, though multi-agent tuning needs practice.

- **Use Case Fit**: Handy in Chapter 3 for testing bot ideas or Chapter 6 for multi-agent prototypes with human oversight.

- **Verdict**: A rapid prototyping champ—use it to brainstorm and test before committing.

LangGraph

- **Ease of Use**: Moderate—pip install langgraph is easy, but graph-based logic requires planning.

- **Scalability**: High—scales well for complex single agents with structured workflows, less so for multi-agent.

- **Multi-Agent Support**: Limited—like LangChain, it's single-agent-focused; multi-agent needs extra effort.

- **Enterprise Readiness**: Moderate—robust for workflows, but lacks enterprise-specific features.

- **Learning Curve**: Medium—graph concepts (nodes, edges) add complexity, builds on LangChain knowledge.

- **Use Case Fit**: Boosts the bot in Chapter 5—structuring decisions (e.g., "if complex, escalate") as a graph.

- **Verdict**: Precision for single-agent workflows—pairs with LangChain for deeper control.

BabyAGI

- **Ease of Use**: High—lightweight, pip install babyagi (or GitHub clone), simple task-driven design.

- **Scalability**: Low—great for small experiments, struggles with large-scale or persistent systems.

- **Multi-Agent Support**: None—single-agent focus, no built-in collaboration.

- **Enterprise Readiness**: Low—minimalist, not built for production or enterprise needs.

- **Learning Curve**: Low—easy to grasp, especially for task prioritization basics.

- **Use Case Fit**: Useful in Chapter 5 for adding task focus to the bot (e.g., prioritize urgent queries).

- **Verdict**: A lean learning tool—good for fundamentals, not production.

Microsoft Copilot

- **Ease of Use**: High—install via VS Code, suggests code instantly, no agent-building overhead.

- **Scalability**: N/A—not a framework, scales with your coding, not the agent itself.

- **Multi-Agent Support**: N/A—supports coding multi-agent logic but doesn't run it.

- **Enterprise Readiness**: High—enterprise-backed (Microsoft), but a dev tool, not a runtime framework.

- **Learning Curve**: Low—plug-and-play for coders, though mastering suggestions takes practice.

- **Use Case Fit**: Speeds up all chapters—e.g., writing ReAct in Chapter 4 or deployment scripts in Chapter 10.

- **Verdict**: A coding booster, not a framework—use it alongside others.

Side-by-Side Comparison Table

Framework	Ease of Use	Scalability	Multi-Agent	Enterprise	Learning Curve	Bot Fit
LangChain	High	Strong	Limited	Moderate	Low	Chapters 4-7
CrewAI	Moderate	High	Excellent	Moderate	Medium	Chapter 6
Semantic Kernel	Low	Very High	Moderate	Excellent	High	Chapter 10
AutoGen	High	Moderate	Strong	Low	Low	Chapter 3, 6
LangGraph	Moderate	High	Limited	Moderate	Medium	Chapter 5
BabyAGI	High	Low	None	Low	Low	Chapter 5
Copilot	High	N/A	N/A	High	Low	All Chapters

Choosing for the Customer Support Bot

- **Start with LangChain**: Its ease, flexibility, and single-agent focus make it the bot's backbone in Chapter 4 (basic FAQs), growing with memory (Chapter 5) and tools (Chapter 7).

- **Add CrewAI**: In Chapter 6, it brings multi-agent collaboration—e.g., a second agent for escalations—building on LangChain.

- **Consider LangGraph**: For Chapter 5, it refines the bot's decision flow if complexity spikes.

- **Use Copilot**: Throughout, it speeds up coding—e.g., suggesting prompts or API calls.

- **Semantic Kernel Later**: In Chapter 10, it's an option for enterprise deployment, though LangChain may suffice with AWS.

- **AutoGen for Testing**: Experiment with it in Chapter 3 to explore bot variants.

- **BabyAGI as a Bonus**: Try it in Chapter 5 for task prioritization, though it's optional.

Why This Matters in 2025

In 2025, picking the right framework can mean the difference between a bot that handles 70% of queries efficiently or one that stumbles. LangChain's simplicity gets you started, CrewAI's teamwork scales it, and Semantic Kernel preps it for big leagues—mirroring industry trends where agents boost productivity by 30%. This comparison ensures you're not just picking a tool but building a strategy.

Next Steps

Chapter 4 dives into LangChain to code the bot's first version—your framework choice starts here. Experiment with others as the project grows.

LangChain, CrewAI, Semantic Kernel, AutoGen, LangGraph, BabyAGI, and Copilot each offer distinct advantages—ease, scale, teamwork, or coding speed. For the bot, LangChain leads, with CrewAI and others stepping in as needed. Armed with this comparison, you're ready to build agents that shine in 2025—let's get to it.

3.4 Exercise: Choose and Install a Framework, Explore Its Documentation

It's time to get hands-on. This exercise puts you in the driver's seat: you'll choose an AI agent framework from LangChain, CrewAI, Microsoft Semantic Kernel, AutoGen, LangGraph, BabyAGI, or Microsoft Copilot, install it in your virtual environment, and dive into its documentation to understand its capabilities. By the end, you'll have a working framework ready for Chapter 4's coding and a solid grasp of how it supports the customer support bot— or any agent you dream up. This is your chance to explore, experiment, and set the stage for building real-world AI solutions in 2025.

Objectives

- Select a framework based on your goals and the bot's needs.

- Install it in your Chapter 2 virtual environment.

- Explore its official documentation to identify key features and examples.

- Run a basic test to confirm it's working.

- Reflect on how it fits the bot project.

Step-by-Step Instructions

Part 1: Choose Your Framework

1. **Review Options** (from Sections 3.1 and 3.3):

   - **LangChain**: Easy, versatile, great for the bot's FAQ start (Chapter 4) and growth (Chapters 5-7).

   - **CrewAI**: Multi-agent focus, ideal for Chapter 6's escalation feature.

   - **Microsoft Semantic Kernel**: Enterprise-ready, suits Chapter 10's deployment.

   - **AutoGen**: Fast prototyping, good for testing bot ideas now.

   - **LangGraph**: Workflow precision, enhances Chapter 5's bot logic.

   - **BabyAGI**: Simple task-driven, optional for Chapter 5.

   - **Microsoft Copilot**: Coding aid, not a runtime framework—use alongside others.

2. **Pick One**: For this book, **LangChain** is recommended as the bot's foundation—it's beginner-friendly and scales with the project. Feel free to choose another (e.g., AutoGen for quick tests) if curious, but LangChain aligns best with Chapter 4's next steps.

3. **Why LangChain?**: It's simple to install, integrates LLMs easily, and supports the bot's evolution—FAQ answers, memory, and tools—all in Python, matching 2025's agent-building trends.

Part 2: Activate Your Virtual Environment

1. **Navigate to Your Project Folder**:

   o If using ai-agent-dev from Chapter 2: cd ai-agent-dev.

2. **Activate**:

   o **Windows**: venv\Scripts\activate

   o **macOS/Linux**: source venv/bin/activate

   o See (venv) in your prompt.

3. **Verify**: python --version (e.g., "Python 3.12.1") and pip --version—both should point to venv.

Part 3: Install the Framework

1. **Install LangChain** (or your chosen framework):

   o pip install langchain

   o Extras: pip install langchain-community (for embeddings, tools) and pip install python-dotenv (for API keys).

   o Others:

      ▪ CrewAI: pip install crewai

      ▪ Semantic Kernel: pip install semantic-kernel

      ▪ AutoGen: pip install pyautogen

      ▪ LangGraph: pip install langgraph

      ▪ BabyAGI: pip install babyagi (or clone from GitHub if unavailable).

      ▪ Copilot: Install via VS Code marketplace, not pip—skip runtime install here.

2. **Check Installation**:

    o pip show langchain—shows version (e.g., 0.1.0) and details.

    o If errors, retry with pip install --upgrade pip then reinstall.

Part 4: Configure API Keys

1. **Ensure Keys Are Set** (from Section 2.2):

    o OpenAI key in .env: OPENAI_API_KEY=sk-abc123... (get from openai.com if needed).

    o Hugging Face token (optional): HUGGINGFACE_TOKEN=hf_xyz789....

    o Verify: python -c "import os; print(os.getenv('OPENAI_API_KEY'))"—shouldn't be None after loading .env.

2. **Why**: LangChain needs an LLM (e.g., OpenAI) to function—keys unlock it.

Part 5: Explore the Documentation

1. **Find the Docs**:

    o **LangChain**: docs.langchain.com (or search "LangChain documentation 2025").

    o **CrewAI**: crewai.com/docs or GitHub (github.com/crewAI).

    o **Semantic Kernel**: microsoft.github.io/Semantic-Kernel.

    o **AutoGen**: microsoft.github.io/autogen.

    o **LangGraph**: langchain-ai.github.io/langgraph.

    o **BabyAGI**: github.com/yoheinakajima/babyagi.

    o **Copilot**: docs.github.com/copilot.

2. **What to Look For** (20-30 minutes):

    o **Quickstart**: Find a "Get Started" section—e.g., LangChain's shows LLM setup.

- Components: Spot LLMs, prompts, chains, agents, tools (Section 3.2).

- Examples: Look for a simple agent (e.g., LangChain's ReAct example).

- API Reference: Note key classes (e.g., OpenAI, Agent in LangChain).

3. **Take Notes**:

- Jot down: How does it initialize an LLM? What's a basic agent look like? Any bot-relevant features (e.g., memory in LangChain)?

- Example: LangChain docs highlight LLMChain for chaining prompts and responses—perfect for FAQs.

Part 6: Test with a Simple Script

1. **Write a Test Script**:

- Create test_framework.py in your folder:

python

```
from dotenv import load_dotenv

import os

from langchain.llms import OpenAI

from langchain.prompts import PromptTemplate

from langchain.chains import LLMChain


# Load API key

load_dotenv()

api_key = os.getenv("OPENAI_API_KEY")

if not api_key:
```

```
    print("Error: No OpenAI API key found!")
    exit()


# Set up LLM
llm = OpenAI(api_key=api_key)


# Create a prompt
prompt = PromptTemplate(
    input_variables=["question"],
    template="You're a support bot. Answer this: {question}"
)


# Build a chain
chain = LLMChain(llm=llm, prompt=prompt)


# Test it
response = chain.run("What's your return policy?")
print("Bot Response:", response)
```
  o   For other frameworks, adapt:
    ▪ **CrewAI**: Define a simple agent role and task.
    ▪ **AutoGen**: Use Assistant class for a quick chat.
    ▪ Skip Copilot—it's a coding aid, not runtime.
2. **Run It**:

- python test_framework.py

- Expected Output (LangChain): "Bot Response: You can return items within 30 days with a receipt."

- If blank/errors: Check API key, internet, or reinstall (pip install langchain --force-reinstall).

Part 7: Reflect

1. **Questions to Answer** (in a notebook or mentally):

    - Did the install go smoothly? Any hiccups?

    - What stood out in the docs (e.g., memory features)?

    - How could this framework help the bot (e.g., LangChain's chains for FAQs)?

    - Would you try another framework next time? Why?

2. **Bot Fit**: For LangChain, note it's ready for Chapter 4's FAQ bot—prompts and chains match the goal.

Troubleshooting

- **Install Fails**: Use pip install --upgrade pip, check Python version (3.12).

- **No Response**: Verify API key in .env, ensure internet's on.

- **Import Errors**: Reinstall (pip install langchain) or check typos.

- **Docs Down**: Use cached versions (e.g., Google "site:docs.langchain.com") or GitHub.

What Success Looks Like

- Framework installed, script runs, and you get a bot-like response.

- You've skimmed the docs, spotting features like LangChain's ReAct or CrewAI's roles.

- You're primed for Chapter 4 with a working tool.

Why This Matters in 2025

Picking and mastering a framework now sets you up for agents that handle 70% of queries or boost productivity by 30%—real-world stakes in 2025. LangChain's ease gets the bot rolling, while exploring docs builds intuition for scaling it later.

You've chosen, installed, and tested a framework—LangChain or otherwise—and peeked into its potential via docs. This isn't just setup; it's your first step into agent-building, readying you for the customer support bot in Chapter 4. With this under your belt, you're not just prepared— you're empowered to create. Nice work—let's keep it rolling!

Chapter 4: Building Basic AI Agents with LangChain

4.1 Introduction to LangChain

LangChain is your gateway to building AI agents with Python, a framework that marries the power of large language models (LLMs) with the flexibility to create autonomous, context-aware systems. As of 2025, it's a cornerstone for developers crafting agents like the customer support bot you'll start building in this chapter. LangChain simplifies integrating LLMs with memory, tools, and structured workflows, making it ideal for everything from answering FAQs to handling dynamic conversations. This section introduces LangChain's purpose, core features, and why it's the perfect launchpad for your agent-building journey—setting the stage for hands-on coding with practical, real-world impact.

What Is LangChain?

LangChain is an open-source Python framework designed to enhance LLMs—like OpenAI's GPT-4 or Hugging Face's models—by adding capabilities they lack alone: memory to recall past interactions, tools to interact with the world, and logic to chain tasks together. Launched in 2022, it's evolved by 2025 into a go-to tool for creating AI agents that don't just chat but *act*. Think of it as the scaffolding that turns a smart chatbot into a full-fledged agent, capable of reasoning, fetching data, and adapting—all within a few lines of Python code.

Core Features

LangChain's strength lies in its modular components, which you'll use throughout this book:

- **LLM Integration**: Connects to LLMs (e.g., OpenAI, local models) for natural language understanding and generation—key for the bot's responses.

- **Prompt Management**: Crafts prompts to steer LLM behavior, like "Answer as a friendly support bot," ensuring relevant, on-brand replies.

- **Chains**: Sequences steps—like prompting an LLM, then formatting its output—into reusable workflows, streamlining complex tasks.

- **Memory**: Adds context retention, so the bot remembers "You asked about shipping last time" (explored in Chapter 5).

- **Tools**: Links agents to external resources—APIs, databases, search engines—letting the bot fetch order status or scrape FAQs (Chapter 7).

- **Agents**: Combines these into autonomous entities that reason and act, using patterns like ReAct (Reasoning + Acting), your starting point here.

Why LangChain for AI Agents?

LangChain shines for several reasons in 2025:

- **Ease of Use**: Install with pip install langchain, and you're coding in minutes—perfect for beginners and pros alike.

- **Flexibility**: Works with any LLM, supports custom tools, and scales from simple bots to intricate systems.

- **Community and Ecosystem**: A thriving community (docs.langchain.com, GitHub) keeps it updated with 2025 trends—multi-modal LLMs, dynamic prompts—plus extensive examples.

- **Practicality**: Powers real-world agents handling 70% of customer queries autonomously, aligning with this book's focus on deployable solutions.

For the customer support bot, LangChain's ability to integrate an LLM with a knowledge base (e.g., FAQs) and later add memory and tools makes it a no-brainer choice.

How It Fits the Customer Support Bot

The bot starts here in Chapter 4 as a basic agent: answering FAQs using an LLM and a prompt, powered by LangChain's ReAct pattern. It'll:

- Take a query ("What's your return policy?").

- Reason through it (match to FAQ data).

- Act (reply "30 days with a receipt"). By Chapter 5, LangChain's memory will track chats; by Chapter 7, tools will fetch live data—all built on this foundation. This mirrors 2025's industry bots, cutting response times and boosting efficiency.

Getting Started with LangChain

You've already installed it in Chapter 2 (pip install langchain) and set up an OpenAI key. LangChain's basic workflow is:

1. **Load an LLM**: Connect to OpenAI or a local model.

2. **Define a Prompt**: Tell it how to respond.

3. **Create a Chain**: Link the prompt to the LLM.

4. **Build an Agent**: Add reasoning and actions.

Here's a sneak peek:

python

```
from langchain.llms import OpenAI

from langchain.prompts import PromptTemplate

from langchain.chains import LLMChain


llm = OpenAI(api_key="your-key")

prompt = PromptTemplate(input_variables=["query"],
template="Answer this: {query}")

chain = LLMChain(llm=llm, prompt=prompt)

print(chain.run("What's the weather like?"))
```
This simple chain is the seed for your bot—Section 4.2 expands it into a full agent.

Why It Matters in 2025

LangChain's rise reflects the demand for practical AI—agents that don't just talk but solve problems. With companies reporting 30% productivity gains from such systems, LangChain's blend of simplicity and power puts you at the forefront. It's not just theory; it's the tool powering the bot that could handle thousands of queries daily by Chapter 10.

Next Steps

Section 4.2 dives into coding your first LangChain agent with ReAct, using these components to answer FAQs. You'll build on this base, adding complexity chapter by chapter.

LangChain is your bridge from raw LLMs to functional AI agents, offering the tools to build the customer support bot and beyond. Its intuitive design, robust features, and real-world relevance make it the perfect starting point for 2025's agent revolution. With this intro, you're ready to code—let's turn concepts into action in the next section.

4.2 Implementing a Simple Agent Using the ReAct Pattern

Now it's time to build your first AI agent—a simple version of the customer support bot—using LangChain and the ReAct (Reasoning + Acting) pattern. This approach lets the agent think through a query and take action, like answering from a predefined FAQ list, laying the groundwork for more advanced features later. As of 2025, ReAct is a staple in agent design for its balance of logic and practicality, and with LangChain, you'll have it running in Python with minimal fuss. This section walks you through coding it step-by-step, so by the end, your bot will handle basic customer questions with confidence.

What Is the ReAct Pattern?

ReAct stands for Reasoning + Acting, a method where an agent:

- **Reasons**: Analyzes the input (e.g., "What's your return policy?") to decide what's needed—look up an answer, clarify, or fetch data.

- **Acts**: Executes the decision, like retrieving "You can return items within 30 days" from a knowledge base. It loops these steps as needed, blending LLM reasoning with actionable steps. In LangChain, ReAct powers agents to go beyond rote responses, making it perfect for the bot's first iteration.

Why Use ReAct for the Bot?

For this simple agent, ReAct keeps things straightforward: it reasons over a customer query and acts by pulling an answer from a static FAQ list. It's the seed for the bot's growth—later, you'll add memory (Chapter 5) and tools (Chapter 7)—and mirrors 2025's real-world bots that handle 70% of queries autonomously. LangChain's ReAct implementation makes this easy, requiring no complex setup beyond what you've done in Chapter 2.

Prerequisites

- Python 3.12, virtual environment, and LangChain installed (pip install langchain langchain-community python-dotenv).

- OpenAI API key in .env (e.g., OPENAI_API_KEY=sk-abc123...) from Section 2.2.

- Basic Python skills—variables, imports, functions.

Step-by-Step Implementation

Step 1: Set Up Your Environment

1. **Activate Your Virtual Environment**:

   o cd ai-agent-dev (or your folder from Chapter 2).

   o Windows: venv\Scripts\activate

   o macOS/Linux: source venv/bin/activate

   o See (venv) in your prompt.

2. **Create a File**: Make simple_agent.py in your project folder.

Step 2: Define the FAQ Knowledge Base

The bot needs something to reason over—a simple FAQ list:

- In simple_agent.py, add:

python

```
# FAQ knowledge base

faqs = {

   "What's your return policy?": "You can return items within 30 days with a
receipt.",

   "How long does shipping take?": "Shipping takes 3-5 business days.",

   "Do you ship internationally?": "Yes, we ship to most countries—check
our website for details."

}
```

Step 3: Load the LLM and Environment

Connect LangChain to OpenAI and load your API key:

- Add:

python

```
from dotenv import load_dotenv

import os

from langchain.llms import OpenAI


# Load environment variables

load_dotenv()

api_key = os.getenv("OPENAI_API_KEY")

if not api_key:

    raise ValueError("OpenAI API key not found in .env!")
```

```
# Initialize the LLM

llm = OpenAI(api_key=api_key, temperature=0.7)  # Temperature
adjusts creativity—0.7 is balanced
```

Step 4: Create a Prompt for ReAct

The prompt tells the LLM how to reason and act using the FAQs:

- Add:

python

```
from langchain.prompts import PromptTemplate


# ReAct prompt template

react_prompt = PromptTemplate(

    input_variables=["query", "faqs"],
```
template="""You're a customer support bot. Use this FAQ list to answer the user's query. If the query isn't in the FAQs, say "I'm not sure, but I can look into that for you!"

FAQs: {faqs}

Query: {query}

Step 1: Reason—think about what the query is asking and how it relates to the FAQs.

Step 2: Act—provide the answer or admit you don't know."""
```
)
```

Step 5: Build the Chain

Link the prompt to the LLM in a chain:

- Add:

python

```
from langchain.chains import LLMChain


# Create the chain
chain = LLMChain(llm=llm, prompt=react_prompt)
```

Step 6: Implement the Agent Logic

Run the chain with a query and the FAQ list:

- Add:

python

```
def run_agent(query):
    # Convert FAQs to a string for the prompt
    faq_text = "¥n".join([f"Q: {k}¥nA: {v}" for k, v in
faqs.items()])
    # Run the chain
    response = chain.run(query=query, faqs=faq_text)
    return response


# Test the agent
if __name__ == "__main__":
    test_queries = [
        "What's your return policy?",
        "How long does shipping take?",
```

```
        "What' s your CEO' s name?"

    ]

    for query in test_queries:

        print(f"\nQuery: {query}")

        print(f"Response: {run_agent(query)}")
```

Step 7: Run and Test

Execute: python simple_agent.py

Expected Output:

Query: What's your return policy?

Response: You can return items within 30 days with a receipt.

Query: How long does shipping take?

Response: Shipping takes 3-5 business days.

Query: What's your CEO's name?

Response: I'm not sure, but I can look into that for you!

> o   The LLM reasons: matches FAQ queries, falls back for
>   unknowns.

How It Works

- **Reasoning**: The prompt instructs the LLM to think about the query's intent and check the FAQs.

- **Acting**: It pulls the matching answer or defaults to "I don't know."

- **LangChain's Role**: The chain ties the prompt and LLM, handling input/output seamlessly.

Customizing the Agent

- **Add FAQs**: Expand the faqs dict with more Q&A pairs.

- **Tweak the Prompt**: Change tone (e.g., "Answer formally") or logic (e.g., "Suggest related FAQs").

- **Adjust Temperature**: Lower to 0.3 for stricter answers, raise to 1.0 for creativity (edit llm).

Troubleshooting

- **No Response**: Check API key in .env, internet connection, or OpenAI credits.

- **Errors**: Ensure all imports are installed (pip install langchain-community if missing).

- **Weird Answers**: Refine the prompt—be explicit (e.g., "Don't make up answers").

Why This Matters for the Bot

This simple ReAct agent is the customer support bot's first version—handling basic queries with a knowledge base, a real-world skill in 2025 where bots manage 70% of interactions. It's the foundation: Chapter 5 adds memory, Chapter 7 brings tools, all building on this core.

Next Steps

Section 4.3 explores enhancing this with more ReAct features—dynamic reasoning, maybe a tool. You'll keep growing it chapter by chapter.

You've built a working AI agent with LangChain and ReAct—reasoning over queries and acting with answers. It's small but mighty, a taste of what's ahead as you scale the bot into a full-fledged support system. With this under your belt, you're not just theorizing—you're coding agents that work. Let's keep pushing!

4.3 Defining Actions and Tools

Your simple ReAct agent from Section 4.2 can answer FAQ-based queries, but to make it truly useful—like a real customer support bot—it needs to *act* beyond just talking. In LangChain, actions and tools extend an agent's capabilities, letting it interact with the world by fetching data, performing tasks, or triggering processes. This section builds on your ReAct foundation, adding a custom tool to look up answers when the FAQ list falls short. By the end, your bot will reason over queries, act with FAQ answers when possible, and use a tool to handle unknowns—setting the stage for more advanced integrations in Chapter 7.

What Are Actions and Tools in LangChain?

- **Actions**: Steps an agent takes after reasoning—like responding with an FAQ or fetching external info. In ReAct, actions follow the "Act" phase.

- **Tools**: External functions or services the agent calls to perform actions—like querying a database, searching the web, or sending a message. Tools give LLMs capabilities they lack natively.

- **Why They Matter**: Without tools, the bot's limited to its FAQ list. With them, it can adapt—crucial for 2025's dynamic support systems handling 70% of queries autonomously.

Goal for This Section

Enhance the bot to:

- Answer from FAQs when it knows the answer.

- Use a mock "lookup" tool for unknown queries (e.g., "What's the CEO's name?").

- Lay groundwork for real tools (e.g., APIs in Chapter 7).

Prerequisites

- Working agent from Section 4.2 (simple_agent.py).

- LangChain installed with extras: pip install langchain langchain-community python-dotenv.

- OpenAI API key in .env.

Step-by-Step Implementation

Step 1: Recap the Base Agent

Your current agent uses a chain with a prompt and FAQ list. Let's modify it to include tools:

- Original simple_agent.py:

python

```
from dotenv import load_dotenv

import os

from langchain.llms import OpenAI

from langchain.prompts import PromptTemplate

from langchain.chains import LLMChain


load_dotenv()

api_key = os.getenv("OPENAI_API_KEY")

llm = OpenAI(api_key=api_key, temperature=0.7)


faqs = {

    "What's your return policy?": "You can return items
within 30 days with a receipt.",

    "How long does shipping take?": "Shipping takes 3-5
business days.",
```

```
"Do you ship internationally?": "Yes, we ship to most
countries—check our website."
}


react_prompt = PromptTemplate(

    input_variables=["query", "faqs"],
```
template="""You're a customer support bot. Use this FAQ list to answer
the user's query. If the query isn't in the FAQs, say "I'm not sure, but I can
look into that for you!"

FAQs: {faqs}

Query: {query}

Step 1: Reason—think about what the query is asking and how it relates
to the FAQs.

Step 2: Act—provide the answer or admit you don't know."""

```
)


chain = LLMChain(llm=llm, prompt=react_prompt)


def run_agent(query):
    faq_text = "\n".join([f"Q: {k}\nA: {v}" for k, v in
faqs.items()])

    response = chain.run(query=query, faqs=faq_text)
```

```
    return response


if __name__ == "__main__":

    queries = ["What's your return policy?", "What's your
CEO's name?"]

    for q in queries:

        print(f"\nQuery: {q}\nResponse: {run_agent(q)}")
```

Step 2: Define a Custom Tool

Create a mock lookup tool to simulate fetching answers:

- Add this before the prompt:

python

```
from langchain.tools import Tool


# Mock lookup tool

def lookup_info(query):

    """Simulates looking up info not in FAQs."""

    mock_db = {

        "What's your CEO's name?": "Our CEO is Jane Doe.",

        "What's today's special offer?": "Today's offer is
10% off all electronics."

    }

    return mock_db.get(query, "Sorry, I couldn't find that
info.")
```

Step 3: Integrate the Tool with the Agent

81

LangChain's ReAct agent uses tools explicitly. Switch from a chain to an agent:

- Replace the chain setup with:

python

```python
from langchain.agents import initialize_agent, AgentType


# Define the tool
tools = [
    Tool(
        name="Lookup",
        func=lookup_info,
        description="Use this to find info not in the FAQs."
    )
]


# Initialize ReAct agent
agent = initialize_agent(
    tools=tools,
    llm=llm,
    agent=AgentType.ZERO_SHOT_REACT_DESCRIPTION,   # ReAct without examples
    verbose=True   # Shows reasoning steps
)
```

Step 4: Update the Prompt and Logic

The agent needs a prompt that encourages tool use:

- Replace the old prompt and run_agent:

python

```
# New run_agent function

def run_agent(query):

    faq_text = "¥n".join([f"Q: {k}¥nA: {v}" for k, v in
faqs.items()])

    input_text = f""""You're a customer support bot with
these FAQs:

    {faq_text}
```

Query: {query}

If the query matches an FAQ, answer directly. If not, use the Lookup tool to find the answer."""

response = agent.run(input_text)

return response

Step 5: Test the Enhanced Agent

- Keep the if __name__ == "__main__": block and run:

  o python simple_agent.py

Expected Output:

Query: What's your return policy?

Response: You can return items within 30 days with a receipt.

Query: What's your CEO's name?

Response: Our CEO is Jane Doe.

- **Verbose Output**: You'll see the agent's steps:

- [Reasoning] The query "What's your CEO's name?" isn't in the FAQs.

- [Action] Using Lookup tool.

[Result] Our CEO is Jane Doe.

How It Works

- **Reasoning**: The agent checks the FAQs first—matches trigger a direct answer.

- **Acting**: For unknowns, it calls the Lookup tool, passing the query.

- **Tool**: The mock function simulates a database lookup, returning a hardcoded answer or a fallback.

- **LangChain Magic**: initialize_agent with ReAct ties it together, letting the LLM decide when to use tools.

Customizing Actions and Tools

- **More Tools**: Add a search_web tool (needs pip install google-search or similar in Chapter 7).

python

```
def search_web(query):
    return f"Web says: {query}—check our site for details."
tools.append(Tool(name="Search", func=search_web,
description="Search online."))
```

- **Dynamic FAQs**: Load from a file:

python

```
with open("faqs.txt", "r") as f:
    faqs = dict(line.strip().split("|") for line in f)
```

- **Fine-Tune**: Adjust verbose=False for cleaner output or tweak LLM temperature.

Troubleshooting

- **Tool Not Used**: Ensure the prompt mentions tools explicitly—LLMs need nudging.

- **Errors**: Check langchain-community is installed (pip install langchain-community).

- **No API Response**: Verify key, internet, or OpenAI status.

Why This Matters for the Bot

This upgrade makes the bot more than an FAQ reader—it's an agent that acts, a step toward 2025's proactive support systems. The Lookup tool is a placeholder—Chapter 7 swaps it for real APIs (e.g., order tracking), but the pattern's the same. You've just unlocked adaptability.

Next Steps

Section 4.4's exercise has you tweak this agent—add FAQs, tools, or queries—cementing your skills before Chapter 5's memory boost.

You've armed your ReAct agent with actions and tools, turning it into a dynamic helper that reasons and fetches answers. This isn't just a bot—it's the start of a real support system, ready to grow with LangChain's power. Nice work—let's keep refining it!

4.4 Handling User Input and Generating Responses

Your ReAct agent from Section 4.3 can reason over queries and use tools, but to truly function as a customer support bot, it needs to interact with users in real-time—taking their input and generating tailored responses. This section enhances the bot to handle dynamic user queries via a command-line interface, process them with LangChain's ReAct pattern, and deliver clear, context-appropriate answers. By the end, you'll have a conversational agent that feels alive, setting the stage for memory (Chapter 5) and external integrations (Chapter 7)—a practical step toward 2025's interactive AI systems.

Why Handle User Input?

Static test queries are fine for prototyping, but real bots face unpredictable questions from users. Handling input means:

- Accepting live queries (e.g., typed in a terminal).

- Processing them with the agent's reasoning and tools.

- Responding naturally, like a human support rep. In 2025, this interactivity is key—bots managing 70% of queries need to adapt on the fly, not just recite scripts.

Goal for This Section

Upgrade the bot to:

- Accept user input via a loop.

- Use the ReAct agent to process it with FAQs and the Lookup tool.

- Generate concise, user-friendly responses.

Prerequisites

- Working agent from Section 4.3 (simple_agent.py).

- LangChain and dependencies installed (pip install langchain langchain-community python-dotenv).

- OpenAI API key in .env.

Step-by-Step Implementation

Step 1: Recap the Current Agent

Here's the base from Section 4.3:

python

```
from dotenv import load_dotenv

import os

from langchain.llms import OpenAI
```

```python
from langchain.tools import Tool
from langchain.agents import initialize_agent, AgentType

load_dotenv()
api_key = os.getenv("OPENAI_API_KEY")
llm = OpenAI(api_key=api_key, temperature=0.7)

faqs = {
    "What's your return policy?": "You can return items within 30 days with a receipt.",
    "How long does shipping take?": "Shipping takes 3-5 business days.",
    "Do you ship internationally?": "Yes, we ship to most countries-check our website."
}

def lookup_info(query):
    mock_db = {
        "What's your CEO's name?": "Our CEO is Jane Doe.",
        "What's today's special offer?": "Today's offer is 10% off all electronics."
    }
    return mock_db.get(query, "Sorry, I couldn't find that info.")
```

```python
tools = [Tool(name="Lookup", func=lookup_info,
description="Use this to find info not in the FAQs.")]


agent = initialize_agent(

    tools=tools,

    llm=llm,

    agent=AgentType.ZERO_SHOT_REACT_DESCRIPTION,

    verbose=True

)


def run_agent(query):
    faq_text = "\n".join([f"Q: {k}\nA: {v}" for k, v in
faqs.items()])

    input_text = f"""You're a customer support bot with
these FAQs:

    {faq_text}


    Query: {query}


    If the query matches an FAQ, answer directly. If not, use
the Lookup tool."""

    return agent.run(input_text)
```

```python
if __name__ == "__main__":

    queries = ["What's your return policy?", "What's your
CEO's name?"]

    for q in queries:

        print(f"\nQuery: {q}\nResponse: {run_agent(q)}")
```

Step 2: Add an Input Loop

Replace the static test block with a conversational loop:

- Update the if __name__ == "__main__": section:

python

```python
if __name__ == "__main__":

    print("Welcome to the Customer Support Bot! Type 'quit'
to exit.")

    while True:

        query = input("Your question: ").strip()

        if query.lower() == "quit":

            print("Goodbye!")

            break

        if not query:

            print("Please ask something!")

            continue

        response = run_agent(query)

        print(f"Bot: {response}")
```

Step 3: Refine the Prompt for Conversation

Tweak the prompt for a friendlier, more natural tone:

- Update run_agent:

python

```python
def run_agent(query):
    faq_text = "\n".join([f"Q: {k}\nA: {v}" for k, v in
faqs.items()])

    input_text = f"""You're a friendly customer support bot.
Use these FAQs to answer:

    {faq_text}


    Query: {query}


If the query matches an FAQ, reply directly and concisely. If not, use the
Lookup tool to find the answer. Keep responses short and helpful."""

    return agent.run(input_text)
```

Step 4: Test the Interactive Bot

Run It: python simple_agent.py

Interact:

Welcome to the Customer Support Bot! Type 'quit' to exit.

Your question: What's your return policy?

Bot: You can return items within 30 days with a receipt.

Your question: What's your CEO's name?

Bot: Our CEO is Jane Doe.

Your question: What's the weather like?

Bot: Sorry, I couldn't find that info.

Your question: quit

Goodbye!

1. **Verbose Output**: You'll see reasoning steps (e.g., "Using Lookup tool")—set verbose=False in initialize_agent for a quieter run.

How It Works

- **Input**: The input() loop captures user queries, exiting on "quit."

- **Processing**: The ReAct agent reasons—checks FAQs, calls Lookup if needed—using the refined prompt.

- **Response**: The LLM generates a short, helpful answer, returned via agent.run().

- **LangChain's Role**: Manages the agent's logic, tools, and LLM interaction seamlessly.

Enhancing the Experience

- **Error Handling**: Add input validation:

python

```
if len(query) > 100:

    print("Bot: Keep it short, please!")

    continue
```

- **Tone**: Adjust prompt (e.g., "Answer formally") or temperature (0.3 for strict, 1.0 for chatty).

- **Feedback**: Add "Did that help? (y/n)" and log responses for Chapter 8's training.

Troubleshooting

- **No Input**: Ensure input() works—test with print(input("Test: ")).

- **Bad Responses**: Check prompt clarity—add "Don't guess" if the LLM fabricates.

- **Tool Fails**: Verify lookup_info logic or tool description in Tool().

Why This Matters for the Bot

This interactive bot is a leap toward real-world use—handling live input mirrors 2025's support systems that cut response times and boost satisfaction. It's still basic (FAQs + mock lookup), but the pattern scales—memory in Chapter 5, APIs in Chapter 7—making it a true agent, not a script.

Next Steps

Section 4.5's exercise has you tweak this—add FAQs, tools, or polish responses—before Chapter 5's memory upgrade.

You've turned your ReAct agent into a conversational powerhouse, taking user input and firing back smart responses with LangChain. This is the customer support bot taking shape—interactive, adaptable, and ready to grow. You're not just coding—you're building a helper that works. Let's polish it next!

4.5 Exercise: Build a Basic AI Agent and Test It with Sample Inputs

This exercise is your chance to put everything from Chapter 4 into action: you'll build a basic AI agent using LangChain and the ReAct pattern, equip it with FAQs and a tool, and make it interactive to handle user input. By the end, you'll have a working customer support bot that responds to sample queries—both predefined and live—proving you can craft a functional agent from scratch. This hands-on task locks in your skills as of 2025, setting you up for Chapter 5's upgrades and beyond. Let's dive in and build something real.

Objectives

- Create a LangChain agent with ReAct to answer FAQs.

- Add a custom tool for queries outside the FAQ list.

- Enable real-time user input via a command-line interface.

- Test it with sample inputs—static and interactive—to ensure it works.

- Reflect on its performance and potential tweaks.

Prerequisites

- Python 3.12, virtual environment, and LangChain installed (pip install langchain langchain-community python-dotenv).

- OpenAI API key in .env (e.g., OPENAI_API_KEY=sk-abc123...) from Chapter 2.

- Code from Sections 4.2-4.4 as a reference.

Step-by-Step Instructions

Part 1: Set Up Your Environment

1. **Activate Your Virtual Environment**:

    o cd ai-agent-dev (or your project folder).

    o Windows: venv\Scripts\activate

    o macOS/Linux: source venv/bin/activate

    o See (venv) in your prompt.

2. **Create a New File**: Make support_bot.py in your folder.

Part 2: Build the Agent

1. **Imports and Setup**:

    o Add to support_bot.py:

python

```
from dotenv import load_dotenv
import os
from langchain.llms import OpenAI
from langchain.tools import Tool
```

```python
from langchain.agents import initialize_agent, AgentType
```

```python
# Load API key
load_dotenv()
api_key = os.getenv("OPENAI_API_KEY")
if not api_key:
    raise ValueError("OpenAI API key not found in .env!")
llm = OpenAI(api_key=api_key, temperature=0.7)
```

2. **Define FAQs**:

   o Add:

python

```python
# FAQ knowledge base
faqs = {
    "What's your return policy?": "You can return items within 30 days with a receipt.",
    "How long does shipping take?": "Shipping takes 3-5 business days.",
    "Do you ship internationally?": "Yes, we ship to most countries-check our website."
}
```

3. **Create a Tool**:

   o Add:

python

```python
# Mock lookup tool
```

```python
def lookup_info(query):
    mock_db = {
        "What's your CEO's name?": "Our CEO is Jane Doe.",
        "What's today's special offer?": "Today's offer is 10% off all electronics."
    }
    return mock_db.get(query, "Sorry, I couldn't find that info.")


tools = [Tool(
    name="Lookup",
    func=lookup_info,
    description="Use this to find info not in the FAQs."
)]
```

4. **Initialize the Agent**:
   o Add:

python

```python
# Set up ReAct agent
agent = initialize_agent(
    tools=tools,
    llm=llm,
    agent=AgentType.ZERO_SHOT_REACT_DESCRIPTION,
    verbose=True  # See reasoning steps
)
```

5. **Handle Input and Responses**:

    o Add:

python

```
def run_agent(query):
    faq_text = "¥n".join([f"Q: {k}¥nA: {v}" for k, v in
faqs.items()])
    input_text = f"""You're a friendly customer support bot.
Use these FAQs:
    {faq_text}
```

Query: {query}

If the query matches an FAQ, reply directly and concisely. If not, use the Lookup tool. Keep answers short and helpful."""

```
    return agent.run(input_text)
```

Part 3: Add Interactive Loop and Tests

1. **Main Block**:

    o Add:

python

```
if __name__ == "__main__":
    # Sample static queries
    sample_queries = [
        "What's your return policy?",
        "How long does shipping take?",
        "What's your CEO's name?",
```

96

```python
        "What's the weather like?"
    ]
    print("Testing with sample queries:")
    for query in sample_queries:
        print(f"\nQuery: {query}")
        print(f"Bot: {run_agent(query)}")


    # Interactive mode
    print("\nNow try it live! Type 'quit' to exit.")
    while True:
        query = input("Your question: ").strip()
        if query.lower() == "quit":
            print("Goodbye!")
            break
        if not query:
            print("Bot: Please ask something!")
            continue
        print(f"Bot: {run_agent(query)}")
```

Part 4: Run and Test

Execute: python support_bot.py

Expected Output:

Testing with sample queries:

Query: What's your return policy?

Bot: You can return items within 30 days with a receipt.

Query: How long does shipping take?

Bot: Shipping takes 3-5 business days.

Query: What's your CEO's name?

Bot: Our CEO is Jane Doe.

Query: What's the weather like?

Bot: Sorry, I couldn't find that info.

Now try it live! Type 'quit' to exit.

Your question: Do you ship internationally?

Bot: Yes, we ship to most countries—check our website.

Your question: quit

Goodbye!

Verbose Logs: You'll see ReAct steps (e.g., "Thought: Query not in FAQs, using Lookup"). Set verbose=False for cleaner output.

Part 5: Customize and Reflect

1. **Tweak It**:

    o Add two new FAQs to faqs (e.g., "What's your store hours?").

    o Expand lookup_info with one more mock answer (e.g., "What's your phone number?").

o   Adjust the prompt tone (e.g., "Answer formally").

2. **Test Again**:

o   Run with your new FAQs and tool entries—e.g., "What's your store hours?"

o   Try edge cases: empty input, gibberish ("xyz").

3. **Reflect** (in a notebook or mentally):

o   Did it handle all queries well?

o   Were responses clear and concise?

o   What could improve (e.g., better fallback, faster replies)?

Troubleshooting

- **No Output**: Check API key, internet, or OpenAI credits.

- **Import Errors**: Reinstall (pip install langchain-community).

- **Tool Skipped**: Ensure prompt mentions "Lookup tool"—LLMs need cues.

- **Weird Replies**: Lower temperature (e.g., 0.3) or tighten the prompt.

What Success Looks Like

- Static tests pass—FAQs and Lookup work as expected.

- Live input flows smoothly—type a query, get a sensible answer.

- You've tweaked it, proving you can adapt the agent.

Why This Matters in 2025

This bot mirrors basic support agents in 2025—handling FAQs and fetching answers boosts efficiency, a skill powering 70% query automation. It's your first real agent, ready to grow with memory and APIs, aligning with industry demands.

You've built and tested a basic AI agent with LangChain—ReAct reasoning, FAQ answers, a tool, and live input. It's not just code; it's a working support bot, your foundation for Chapter 5's memory and beyond. You're now an agent builder—great job! Keep experimenting as you move forward.

Chapter 5: Advanced Agent Development

Welcome to the next level of AI agent creation. In Chapter 4, you built a basic customer support bot with LangChain and the ReAct pattern, capable of answering FAQs and using a simple tool. Now, in Chapter 5, we'll push that agent further, adding advanced features to make it smarter, more responsive, and closer to real-world systems as of 2025. You'll explore memory to track conversations, enhance decision-making with complex logic, and customize the bot for specific needs—transforming it from a basic responder into a dynamic, context-aware assistant. This chapter is where your agent starts to shine, handling the nuances that make AI truly valuable in today's automated world.

5.1 Memory Management and Stateful Agents

Your customer support bot from Chapter 4 can answer queries and use tools, but it's forgetful—each question is a fresh start, with no memory of past interactions. In this section, you'll add memory management using LangChain, turning it into a *stateful agent* that remembers conversations and uses context to give smarter, more relevant responses. By the end, your bot will recall what users asked before—like "You mentioned shipping earlier, need an update?"—bringing it closer to the advanced, context-aware systems powering 2025's AI-driven support. Let's dive into memory and make your agent truly conversational.

Why Memory Matters

Without memory, the bot treats every query in isolation, missing the flow of a real conversation. Memory lets it:

- Track history: "You asked about returns last time—still need help?"

- Personalize: "Since you're international, shipping takes 3-5 days."

- Avoid repetition: No need to re-explain what's already covered. In 2025, stateful agents are key to handling 70% of queries autonomously—context is king, and LangChain makes it easy to add.

What Is a Stateful Agent?

A stateful agent maintains a "state"—data about past interactions—across queries. In LangChain, this state is memory, stored as conversation history, which the agent uses to inform its reasoning and actions. Unlike the stateless bot from Chapter 4, a stateful one remembers, making it feel more human and useful.

Types of Memory in LangChain

LangChain offers flexible memory options:

- **ConversationBufferMemory**: Stores the full chat history—simple but grows large.

- **ConversationSummaryMemory**: Summarizes past chats—compact, good for long sessions.

- **ConversationBufferWindowMemory**: Keeps a fixed window (e.g., last 5 exchanges)—balanced for most cases. For the bot, we'll start with ConversationBufferMemory—it's straightforward and fits short support chats.

Goal for This Section

Upgrade the bot to:

- Store and recall conversation history.

- Use that context in ReAct reasoning (e.g., "You asked X before, so here's Y").

- Maintain state across an interactive session.

Prerequisites

- Working bot from Chapter 4 (support_bot.py).

- LangChain installed (pip install langchain langchain-community python-dotenv).

- OpenAI API key in .env.

Step-by-Step Implementation

Step 1: Recap the Base Agent

Here's the Chapter 4 bot (support_bot.py):

python

```
from dotenv import load_dotenv

import os

from langchain.llms import OpenAI

from langchain.tools import Tool

from langchain.agents import initialize_agent, AgentType


load_dotenv()

api_key = os.getenv("OPENAI_API_KEY")

llm = OpenAI(api_key=api_key, temperature=0.7)


faqs = {

    "What's your return policy?": "You can return items
within 30 days with a receipt.",

    "How long does shipping take?": "Shipping takes 3-5
business days.",

    "Do you ship internationally?": "Yes, we ship to most
countries—check our website."

}


def lookup_info(query):
```

```python
    mock_db = {
        "What's your CEO's name?": "Our CEO is Jane Doe.",
        "What's today's special offer?": "Today's offer is
10% off all electronics."
    }
    return mock_db.get(query, "Sorry, I couldn't find that
info.")


tools = [Tool(name="Lookup", func=lookup_info,
description="Use this to find info not in the FAQs.")]


agent = initialize_agent(
    tools=tools,
    llm=llm,
    agent=AgentType.ZERO_SHOT_REACT_DESCRIPTION,
    verbose=True
)


def run_agent(query):
    faq_text = "\n".join([f"Q: {k}\nA: {v}" for k, v in
faqs.items()])

    input_text = f"""You're a friendly customer support bot.
Use these FAQs:

    {faq_text}
```

Query: {query}

If the query matches an FAQ, reply directly and concisely. If not, use the Lookup tool."""

    return agent.run(input_text)

```python
if __name__ == "__main__":
    print("Welcome to the Customer Support Bot! Type 'quit' to exit.")
    while True:
        query = input("Your question: ").strip()
        if query.lower() == "quit":
            print("Goodbye!")
            break
        if not query:
            print("Bot: Please ask something!")
            continue
        print(f"Bot: {run_agent(query)}")
```

Step 2: Add Memory to the Agent

Import memory and integrate it:

- Update imports and agent setup:

python

```python
from langchain.memory import ConversationBufferMemory
```

```python
# Initialize memory

memory = ConversationBufferMemory()


# Update agent with memory

agent = initialize_agent(

    tools=tools,

    llm=llm,

    agent=AgentType.ZERO_SHOT_REACT_DESCRIPTION,

    memory=memory,   # Add memory here

    verbose=True

)
```

Step 3: Refine the Prompt for Context

Adjust the prompt to use memory:

- Update run_agent:

python

```python
def run_agent(query):

    faq_text = "\n".join([f"Q: {k}\nA: {v}" for k, v in faqs.items()])

    input_text = f"""You're a friendly customer support bot. Use these FAQs:

    {faq_text}
```

Use the conversation history to provide context-aware answers when relevant.

Query: {query}

If the query matches an FAQ, reply directly and concisely. If not, use the Lookup tool. Keep answers short and helpful."""

```
    return agent.run(input_text)
```

Step 4: Test the Stateful Agent

Run: python support_bot.py

Interact:

Welcome to the Customer Support Bot! Type 'quit' to exit.

Your question: How long does shipping take?

Bot: Shipping takes 3-5 business days.

Your question: What about international?

Bot: Since you asked about shipping, I assume you mean international shipping—yes, we ship to most countries, check our website.

Your question: Who's your CEO?

Bot: Our CEO is Jane Doe.

Your question: quit

Goodbye!

1. **Verbose Output**: See reasoning like:

2. [Thought] User asked about shipping before, so "international" likely means shipping.

[Action] Answer from FAQs with context.

How It Works

- **Memory**: ConversationBufferMemory stores each query and response, passing the history to the LLM with every call.

- **Reasoning**: The LLM uses the prompt and history to connect dots (e.g., "international" relates to prior shipping talk).

- **Acting**: It pulls from FAQs, tools, or context-aware logic.

- **LangChain**: Ties memory to the ReAct agent seamlessly.

Customizing Memory

- **Window Memory**: Limit to last 3 exchanges:

python

```
from langchain.memory import ConversationBufferWindowMemory

memory = ConversationBufferWindowMemory(k=3)
```

- **Summary Memory**: Summarize instead:

python

```
from langchain.memory import ConversationSummaryMemory

memory = ConversationSummaryMemory(llm=llm)
```

- **Clear Memory**: Reset with memory.clear() (e.g., per session).

Troubleshooting

- **No Context**: Ensure memory is passed to initialize_agent and prompt mentions history.

- **Memory Overload**: Switch to window or summary if chats grow too long.

- **Errors**: Check LangChain version (pip install --upgrade langchain).

Why This Matters for the Bot

Memory turns the bot into a conversational partner, not a reset button. In 2025, this is table stakes—context-aware bots save time and boost satisfaction, handling follow-ups like pros. It's the first big leap toward a production-ready agent.

You've made your bot stateful with memory, letting it recall and leverage past chats. This isn't just an upgrade—it's a game-changer, aligning with 2025's demand for intelligent agents. With LangChain's memory in play, you're ready to tackle bigger challenges—let's keep building!

5.2 Handling Complex Tasks and Decision-Making

Your customer support bot now remembers conversations thanks to memory from Section 5.1, but it's still limited to simple FAQ lookups and basic tool use. In this section, you'll enhance it to handle complex tasks and make smarter decisions—reasoning through multi-step queries, choosing between multiple tools, and escalating issues when needed. Using LangChain's ReAct pattern, you'll add logic to process nuanced requests like "Can you check my order and explain the return policy?"—bringing the bot closer to the sophisticated agents driving 2025's automation revolution. Let's level up its decision-making power.

Why Complex Tasks and Decision-Making?

Real-world support isn't just "yes/no" answers—it's messy:

- Multi-part queries: "Track my order and tell me about returns."

- Conditional logic: "If it's late, escalate; if not, reassure."

- Tool selection: "Use tracking API or FAQ lookup?" In 2025, agents managing 70% of queries need to juggle these, boosting efficiency by 30% in firms like Salesforce. This section makes your bot that smart.

Goal for This Section

Upgrade the bot to:

- Process complex, multi-step queries.

- Decide between tools (e.g., FAQ, lookup, or mock escalation).

- Use ReAct to reason through decisions and act accordingly.

Prerequisites

- Working bot from Section 5.1 (support_bot.py) with memory.

- LangChain installed (pip install langchain langchain-community python-dotenv).

- OpenAI API key in .env.

Step-by-Step Implementation

Step 1: Recap the Stateful Agent

Here's the base from Section 5.1:

python

```
from dotenv import load_dotenv

import os

from langchain.llms import OpenAI

from langchain.tools import Tool

from langchain.agents import initialize_agent, AgentType

from langchain.memory import ConversationBufferMemory


load_dotenv()

api_key = os.getenv("OPENAI_API_KEY")

llm = OpenAI(api_key=api_key, temperature=0.7)


faqs = {

    "What's your return policy?": "You can return items within 30 days with a receipt.",
```

```python
    "How long does shipping take?": "Shipping takes 3-5
business days.",

    "Do you ship internationally?": "Yes, we ship to most
countries-check our website."
}


def lookup_info(query):
    mock_db = {
        "What's your CEO's name?": "Our CEO is Jane Doe.",

        "What's today's special offer?": "Today's offer is
10% off all electronics."
    }

    return mock_db.get(query, "Sorry, I couldn't find that
info.")


tools = [Tool(name="Lookup", func=lookup_info,
description="Use this to find info not in the FAQs.")]


memory = ConversationBufferMemory()
agent = initialize_agent(
    tools=tools,
    llm=llm,
    agent=AgentType.ZERO_SHOT_REACT_DESCRIPTION,
    memory=memory,
```

```python
        verbose=True
)


def run_agent(query):
    faq_text = "¥n".join([f"Q: {k}¥nA: {v}" for k, v in
faqs.items()])

    input_text = f"""You're a friendly customer support bot.
Use these FAQs:

    {faq_text}


    Use the conversation history to provide context-aware
answers when relevant.

    Query: {query}


    If the query matches an FAQ, reply directly and
concisely. If not, use the Lookup tool."""

    return agent.run(input_text)


if __name__ == "__main__":

    print("Welcome to the Customer Support Bot! Type 'quit'
to exit.")
    while True:

        query = input("Your question: ").strip()

        if query.lower() == "quit":
```

```python
        print("Goodbye!")

        break

    if not query:

        print("Bot: Please ask something!")

        continue

    print(f"Bot: {run_agent(query)}")
```

Step 2: Add More Tools

Introduce tools for complex tasks:

- Add before tools definition:

python

```python
def check_order_status(query):

    """Mock order status checker."""

    if "order" in query.lower():

        return "Your order #123 is in transit, expected
delivery in 2 days."

    return "Please provide an order-related query."


def escalate_issue(query):

    """Mock escalation tool."""

    return f"I've escalated '{query}' to a human agent-
someone will follow up soon."
```

- Update tools:

python

```python
tools = [
```

```
    Tool(name="Lookup", func=lookup_info, description="Find
info not in FAQs."),

    Tool(name="OrderStatus", func=check_order_status,
description="Check order status for order-related queries."),

    Tool(name="Escalate", func=escalate_issue,
description="Escalate complex or urgent issues to a human.")
]
```

Step 3: Enhance the Prompt for Decision-Making

Update the prompt to handle complexity:

- Modify run_agent:

python

```python
def run_agent(query):

    faq_text = "¥n".join([f"Q: {k}¥nA: {v}" for k, v in
faqs.items()])

    input_text = f"""You're a friendly customer support bot.
Use these FAQs:

    {faq_text}
```

Use conversation history for context. Query: {query}

Reason through the query step-by-step:

1. If it matches an FAQ, answer directly.

2. If it's about an order (e.g., 'track', 'status'), use OrderStatus tool.

3. If it's complex, urgent, or unclear (e.g., 'help now', 'broken'), use Escalate tool.

4. For anything else, use Lookup tool.

Keep answers short, helpful, and context-aware."""

   return agent.run(input_text)

Step 4: Test Complex Queries

Run: python support_bot.py

Interact:

Welcome to the Customer Support Bot! Type 'quit' to exit.

Your question: What's your return policy?

Bot: You can return items within 30 days with a receipt.

Your question: Can you track my order?

Bot: Your order #123 is in transit, expected delivery in 2 days.

Your question: My package is broken—help now!

Bot: I've escalated 'My package is broken—help now!' to a human agent—someone will follow up soon.

Your question: What's today's special offer?

Bot: Today's offer is 10% off all electronics.

Your question: Can you check my order and explain returns?

Bot: Your order #123 is in transit, expected in 2 days. Returns are allowed within 30 days with a receipt.

Your question: quit

Goodbye!

Verbose Output: See steps like:

[Thought] Query has 'order' and 'returns'—multi-step.

[Action] Use OrderStatus, then FAQ.

How It Works

- **Tools**: Three options—FAQ lookup, order status, escalation—give the agent flexibility.

- **Reasoning**: The prompt guides the LLM to analyze the query (e.g., "multi-part" or "urgent") and pick tools.

- **Acting**: ReAct loops through decisions—FAQ first, then tools as needed.

- **Memory**: Context from prior queries (e.g., "order" mention) informs responses.

- **LangChain**: Orchestrates tools, memory, and LLM seamlessly.

Customizing Decision-Making

- **More Tools**: Add a search_web tool for unknowns (Chapter 7 prep).

- **Logic**: Tweak prompt—e.g., "Escalate if 'urgent' or over 20 words."

- **Fallback**: Add "Ask me to clarify" if no tool fits.

Troubleshooting

- **Wrong Tool**: Refine prompt—be explicit (e.g., "Use OrderStatus for 'track'").

- **No Action**: Check tool descriptions—vague ones confuse the LLM.

- **Memory Clash**: Clear with memory.clear() if testing breaks context.

Why This Matters for the Bot

Complex tasks and decisions make the bot a problem-solver, not just a talker—vital for 2025's 30% productivity boosts. It's now handling multi-step queries and escalation, mimicking real support agents.

Next Steps

Section 5.3 customizes it for specific domains—your smart bot gets a personality.

You've supercharged your bot with complex task handling and decision-making—multi-tool reasoning, context from memory, and ReAct logic. This is advanced agent territory, ready for real-world challenges. Great work—let's tailor it next!

5.3 Customizing Agent Behavior

Your customer support bot is now stateful and adept at complex tasks, thanks to memory and enhanced decision-making from Sections 5.1 and 5.2. But to make it truly shine, it needs personality and purpose—custom behavior tailored to specific needs, like a bookstore's support bot versus a generic one. In this section, you'll customize the bot's tone, scope, and logic using LangChain, shaping it into a specialized agent that fits a unique domain. By the end, your bot will feel purpose-built—friendly, focused, and fine-tuned—mirroring the bespoke AI systems thriving in 2025's automation landscape.

Why Customize Behavior?

A generic bot is useful, but customization makes it *relevant*:

- **Tone**: Friendly for retail, formal for finance.

- **Scope**: Focus on books, not electronics, for a bookstore.

- **Logic**: Prioritize store-specific queries over generic ones. In 2025, tailored agents drive user satisfaction and efficiency—think a bot that knows your business inside out, boosting productivity by 30%. LangChain's flexibility lets you mold the bot to any niche.

Goal for This Section

Customize the bot to:

- Act as a bookstore support agent with a friendly, bookish tone.

- Use bookstore-specific FAQs and tools.

- Adjust reasoning to prioritize book-related queries.

Prerequisites

- Working bot from Section 5.2 (support_bot.py) with memory and tools.

- LangChain installed (pip install langchain langchain-community python-dotenv).

- OpenAI API key in .env.

Step-by-Step Implementation

Step 1: Recap the Current Agent

Here's the base from Section 5.2:

python

```
from dotenv import load_dotenv

import os

from langchain.llms import OpenAI

from langchain.tools import Tool

from langchain.agents import initialize_agent, AgentType

from langchain.memory import ConversationBufferMemory


load_dotenv()

api_key = os.getenv("OPENAI_API_KEY")

llm = OpenAI(api_key=api_key, temperature=0.7)


faqs = {

    "What's your return policy?": "You can return items
within 30 days with a receipt.",
```

```python
    "How long does shipping take?": "Shipping takes 3-5
business days.",

    "Do you ship internationally?": "Yes, we ship to most
countries-check our website."
}


def lookup_info(query):
    mock_db = {
        "What's your CEO's name?": "Our CEO is Jane Doe.",

        "What's today's special offer?": "Today's offer is
10% off all electronics."
    }

    return mock_db.get(query, "Sorry, I couldn't find that
info.")


def check_order_status(query):
    if "order" in query.lower():
        return "Your order #123 is in transit, expected
delivery in 2 days."
    return "Please provide an order-related query."


def escalate_issue(query):
    return f"I've escalated '{query}' to a human agent-
someone will follow up soon."
```

```
tools = [

    Tool(name="Lookup", func=lookup_info, description="Find
info not in FAQs."),

    Tool(name="OrderStatus", func=check_order_status,
description="Check order status."),

    Tool(name="Escalate", func=escalate_issue,
description="Escalate complex or urgent issues.")

]


memory = ConversationBufferMemory()

agent = initialize_agent(

    tools=tools,

    llm=llm,

    agent=AgentType.ZERO_SHOT_REACT_DESCRIPTION,

    memory=memory,

    verbose=True

)


def run_agent(query):

    faq_text = "¥n".join([f"Q: {k}¥nA: {v}" for k, v in
faqs.items()])

    input_text = f"""You're a friendly customer support bot.
Use these FAQs:
```

```
{faq_text}

Use conversation history for context. Query: {query}

Reason through the query step-by-step:

1. If it matches an FAQ, answer directly.

2. If it's about an order (e.g., 'track', 'status'), use OrderStatus tool.

3. If it's complex, urgent, or unclear (e.g., 'help now', 'broken'), use
Escalate tool.

4. For anything else, use Lookup tool.

Keep answers short, helpful, and context-aware."""

return agent.run(input_text)


if __name__ == "__main__":
    print("Welcome to the Customer Support Bot! Type 'quit' to exit.")
    while True:
        query = input("Your question: ").strip()
        if query.lower() == "quit":
            print("Goodbye!")
            break
        if not query:
            print("Bot: Please ask something!")
            continue
        print(f"Bot: {run_agent(query)}")
```

Step 2: Customize FAQs for a Bookstore

Update the knowledge base:

- Replace faqs:

python

```python
faqs = {
    "What's your return policy for books?": "You can return
books within 30 days, in unread condition.",

    "How long does shipping take for books?": "Book shipping
takes 3-5 business days in the US.",

    "Do you ship books internationally?": "Yes, we ship books
worldwide-rates vary by country.",

    "What's your best-seller this week?": "This week's
best-seller is 'The Cosmic Library' by A. Reader."
}
```

Step 3: Tailor Tools for Bookstore Use

Adjust tools to fit:

- Update lookup_info and add a book-specific tool:

python

```python
def lookup_book_info(query):
    mock_book_db = {
        "What's in stock?": "We've got 'The Cosmic
Library' and 'Python Tales' in stock.",

        "Any book deals today?": "Today, buy 2 books and get
10% off!"
    }

    return mock_book_db.get(query, "I couldn't find that-try
asking about specific books!")
```

```python
def check_order_status(query):

    if "order" in query.lower():

        return "Your book order #123 is on its way-expect it
in 2 days."

    return "Ask about a book order, and I'll check!"


def escalate_issue(query):

    return f"Escalated '{query}' to our bookstore staff-
expect a reply soon!"


tools = [

    Tool(name="BookLookup", func=lookup_book_info,
description="Find bookstore-specific info."),

    Tool(name="OrderStatus", func=check_order_status,
description="Check book order status."),

    Tool(name="Escalate", func=escalate_issue,
description="Escalate book-related issues.")

]
```

Step 4: Adjust Prompt for Bookstore Tone and Logic

Make it friendly and book-focused:

- Update run_agent:

python

```python
def run_agent(query):
```

```
    faq_text = "¥n".join([f"Q: {k}¥nA: {v}" for k, v in
faqs.items()])

    input_text = f"""You're a friendly bookstore support
bot-love books and help readers! Use these FAQs:

    {faq_text}
```

Use conversation history for context. Query: {query}

Reason step-by-step:

1. If it matches a book FAQ, answer directly with a bookish flair.

2. If it's about a book order ('track', 'status'), use OrderStatus.

3. If it's complex or urgent ('lost book', 'urgent'), use Escalate.

4. For other book questions, use BookLookup.

If it's not book-related, say "I'm all about books—ask me something bookish!"

Keep answers short, cheerful, and book-loving."""

return agent.run(input_text)

Step 5: Test the Customized Bot

Run: python support_bot.py

Interact:

Welcome to the Customer Support Bot! Type 'quit' to exit.

Your question: What's your return policy for books?

Bot: You can return books within 30 days, as long as they're unread—happy reading!

Your question: Can you track my order?

Bot: Your book order #123 is on its way—expect it in 2 days!

Your question: Lost my book—urgent!

Bot: Escalated 'Lost my book—urgent!' to our bookstore staff—expect a reply soon!

Your question: What's in stock?

Bot: We've got 'The Cosmic Library' and 'Python Tales' in stock—great picks!

Your question: What's the weather like?

Bot: I'm all about books—ask me something bookish!

Your question: quit

Goodbye!

Verbose Output: See steps like:

[Thought] 'track my order' is book-order related.

[Action] Use OrderStatus.

How It Works

- **FAQs**: Book-specific, shaping the bot's core knowledge.

- **Tools**: Tailored for bookstore tasks—stock checks, order status, escalation.

- **Prompt**: Sets a friendly, book-loving tone and prioritizes book queries.

- **Memory**: Ties it together—e.g., "You asked about shipping books before."

- **LangChain**: Flexibly adapts to the new domain via prompt and tools.

Further Customization

- **Tone**: Change to formal—"Returns are accepted within 30 days, madam/sir."

- **Domain**: Swap to tech support—FAQs about gadgets, tools for warranties.

- **Logic**: Add "If asked twice, escalate" with memory checks.

Troubleshooting

- **Off-Topic Answers**: Tighten prompt—e.g., "Stay book-focused."

- **Tool Misuse**: Clarify descriptions—e.g., "BookLookup only for stock/deals."

- **Slow Response**: Lower temperature (e.g., 0.5) for focus.

Why This Matters for the Bot

Customization makes the bot a specialist—not a generic helper, but a bookstore buddy. In 2025, tailored agents boost satisfaction by fitting the user's world, a key to real-world success.

Next Steps

Section 5.4's exercise ties memory, decisions, and customization into a full test.

You've customized your bot into a cheerful bookstore agent—book-specific FAQs, tools, and tone, all powered by LangChain. It's now a unique, context-aware helper, ready for 2025's demands. Awesome work—let's test it next!

5.4 Exercise: Implement Memory in Your Agent and Test Stateful Behavior

This exercise pulls together everything from Chapter 5—memory, complex decision-making, and customized behavior—into a hands-on challenge.

You'll take your customer support bot, add memory to make it stateful, enhance its decision-making with multiple tools, and customize it for a specific domain (e.g., a bookstore). Then, you'll test it with sample inputs to ensure it remembers conversations and responds contextually. By the end, you'll have a robust, advanced agent that mirrors 2025's real-world systems—proving you can build AI that's smart, adaptive, and purpose-driven.

Objectives

- Add ConversationBufferMemory to track chat history.

- Implement multiple tools and decision logic for complex queries.

- Customize the bot for a bookstore with tailored FAQs, tools, and tone.

- Test with static and live inputs to verify stateful behavior.

- Reflect on its performance and potential improvements.

Prerequisites

- Python 3.12, virtual environment, and LangChain installed (pip install langchain langchain-community python-dotenv).

- OpenAI API key in .env (e.g., OPENAI_API_KEY=sk-abc123...).

- Base bot from Chapter 4 or 5 as a starting point.

Step-by-Step Instructions

Part 1: Set Up Your Environment

1. **Activate Virtual Environment**:

    o   cd ai-agent-dev (or your folder).

    o   Windows: venv\Scripts\activate

    o   macOS/Linux: source venv/bin/activate

    o   See (venv) in prompt.

2. **Create a File**: Make advanced_bot.py in your folder.

Part 2: Build the Advanced Agent

1. **Imports and Setup**:

   o Add:

python

```python
from dotenv import load_dotenv

import os

from langchain.llms import OpenAI

from langchain.tools import Tool

from langchain.agents import initialize_agent, AgentType

from langchain.memory import ConversationBufferMemory


load_dotenv()

api_key = os.getenv("OPENAI_API_KEY")

if not api_key:

    raise ValueError("OpenAI API key not found!")

llm = OpenAI(api_key=api_key, temperature=0.7)
```

2. **Custom FAQs (Bookstore)**:

   o Add:

python

```python
faqs = {

    "What's your return policy for books?": "Returns within
30 days, unread condition.",
```

"How long does shipping take for books?": "3-5 business days in the US.",

"Do you ship books internationally?": "Yes, worldwide—rates vary by country.",

"What's your best-seller this week?": " 'The Cosmic Library' by A. Reader."

}

3. **Define Tools**:

    o Add:

python

```python
def lookup_book_info(query):
    mock_db = {
        "What's in stock?": " 'The Cosmic Library'  and 'Python Tales'  are in stock.",
        "Any book deals today?": "Buy 2 books, get 10% off today!"
    }
    return mock_db.get(query, "No info—ask about books!")


def check_order_status(query):
    if "order" in query.lower():
        return "Order #123 is on its way—expect it in 2 days."
    return "Ask about a book order!"
```

```python
def escalate_issue(query):
    return f"Escalated '{query}' to bookstore staff-stay tuned!"


tools = [
    Tool(name="BookLookup", func=lookup_book_info,
description="Find bookstore info."),
    Tool(name="OrderStatus", func=check_order_status,
description="Check book orders."),
    Tool(name="Escalate", func=escalate_issue,
description="Escalate book issues.")
]
```

4. **Add Memory and Agent**:

   o Add:

python

```python
memory = ConversationBufferMemory()
agent = initialize_agent(
    tools=tools,
    llm=llm,
    agent=AgentType.ZERO_SHOT_REACT_DESCRIPTION,
    memory=memory,
    verbose=True
)
```

5. **Handle Queries**:

   o Add:

python

```python
def run_agent(query):

    faq_text = "¥n".join([f"Q: {k}¥nA: {v}" for k, v in
faqs.items()])

    input_text = f"""You're a friendly bookstore bot—mad
about books! Use these FAQs:

    {faq_text}
```

Use chat history for context. Query: {query}

Reason step-by-step:

1. If it's an FAQ, answer with bookish cheer.

2. If it's an order ('track', 'status'), use OrderStatus.

3. If it's urgent or complex ('lost', 'urgent'), use Escalate.

4. For other book queries, use BookLookup.

Non-book stuff? Say "I'm book-obsessed—ask me about reading!"

Keep it short and fun."""

```python
    return agent.run(input_text)
```

Part 3: Test with Sample Inputs

1. **Main Block**:

    o   Add:

python

```python
if __name__ == "__main__":

    # Static tests

    sample_queries = [
```

```python
        "What's your return policy for books?",

        "Can you track my order?",

        "What's in stock?",

        "My book is lost—help fast!",

        "What's the weather?"

    ]

    print("Testing static queries:")

    for query in sample_queries:

        print(f"\nQuery: {query}")

        print(f"Bot: {run_agent(query)}")


    # Live mode

    print("\nLive mode! Type 'quit' to exit.")

    while True:

        query = input("Your question: ").strip()

        if query.lower() == "quit":

            print("Happy reading—bye!")

            break

        if not query:

            print("Bot: Got a book question? Ask away!")

            continue

        print(f"Bot: {run_agent(query)}")
```

Part 4: Run and Verify

Execute: python advanced_bot.py

Expected Output:

Testing static queries:

Query: What's your return policy for books?

Bot: Returns within 30 days, unread condition—keep those pages crisp!

Query: Can you track my order?

Bot: Order #123 is on its way—expect it in 2 days.

Query: What's in stock?

Bot: 'The Cosmic Library' and 'Python Tales' are in stock—great reads!

Query: My book is lost—help fast!

Bot: Escalated 'My book is lost—help fast!' to bookstore staff—stay tuned!

Query: What's the weather?

Bot: I'm book-obsessed—ask me about reading!

Live mode! Type 'quit' to exit.

Your question: How long does shipping take for books?

Bot: 3-5 business days in the US—your next read's coming soon!

Your question: And internationally?

Bot: Since you asked about shipping, I'll assume books—yes, worldwide, rates vary!

Your question: quit

Happy reading—bye!

Part 5: Customize and Reflect

1. **Tweak It**:

   o Add an FAQ: "Do you sell e-books?" → "Yes, e-books are on our site!"

   o Add to lookup_book_info: "Who wrote 'Python Tales'?" → "That's by Code Master."

   o Change tone: Try "formal" in the prompt—e.g., "Answer with bookstore courtesy."

2. **Test Again**:

   o Static: "Do you sell e-books?"

   o Live: "How long does shipping take?" then "What's my order status?"

3. **Reflect**:

   o Did memory work (e.g., context from "shipping" to "internationally")?

   o Were decisions smart (FAQ vs. tool)?

   o How's the bookstore vibe—fun enough?

   o Ideas to improve (e.g., more tools, tighter logic)?

Troubleshooting

- **No Memory**: Check memory in initialize_agent and "history" in prompt.

- **Wrong Tool**: Refine prompt steps—e.g., "Use OrderStatus only for 'order'."

- **Slow**: Lower temperature (e.g., 0.5) or disable verbose.

- **Errors**: Reinstall (pip install --upgrade langchain).

What Success Looks Like

- Static tests pass—FAQs, tools, and fallbacks work.

- Live mode recalls context—e.g., links "shipping" queries.

- Bookstore feel is clear—cheerful and focused.

Why This Matters in 2025

A stateful, customized bot with smart decisions is 2025-ready—handling 70% of queries with context and flair. It's your proof you can build advanced AI that fits real needs.

You've crafted an advanced agent—memory tracks chats, tools tackle complexity, and bookstore charm shines. This isn't just a bot; it's a glimpse of 2025's AI future. Awesome job—keep pushing its limits!

Chapter 6: Multi-Agent Systems

Welcome to Chapter 6, where your AI agent journey scales up from a single, capable bot to a team of collaborating agents—a multi-agent system. In Chapter 5, you built an advanced customer support bot with memory, decision-making, and customization. Now, you'll design and implement a system where multiple agents work together, each with specialized roles, to handle complex tasks like answering queries, tracking orders, and escalating issues. Using frameworks like CrewAI (and a touch of LangChain), you'll create a coordinated team that mirrors 2025's real-world support systems, boosting efficiency and tackling problems no single agent could alone.

Why Multi-Agent Systems?

A single agent is powerful, but it has limits—handling everything from FAQs to escalations can overload it or dilute its focus. Multi-agent systems:

- **Specialize**: One agent answers FAQs, another tracks orders, a third escalates.

- **Collaborate**: Agents share info and hand off tasks seamlessly.

- **Scale**: Teams handle more volume and complexity, like 70% of queries in modern firms. In 2025, multi-agent setups drive 30% productivity gains by dividing labor—think a call center with experts, but AI-powered.

What You'll Learn

- **Design**: Plan a system with distinct agent roles (Section 6.1).

- **Implementation**: Build it with CrewAI and integrate with LangChain (Section 6.1).

- **Coordination**: Enable agent communication and task handoffs (Section 6.2).

- **Exercise**: Test the system with realistic scenarios (Section 6.3).

How It Fits the Customer Support Bot

Your bot becomes a team:

- **FAQ Agent**: Answers basic queries (e.g., "What's the return policy?").

- **Order Agent**: Tracks orders (e.g., "Where's my package?").

- **Escalation Agent**: Handles complex issues (e.g., "My book's lost!"). They'll work together, passing tasks as needed—e.g., FAQ Agent hands off to Order Agent for "Track my return."

Prerequisites

- Bot from Chapter 5 (advanced_bot.py).

- LangChain and CrewAI installed (pip install langchain langchain-community crewai python-dotenv).

- OpenAI API key in .env.

6.1 Designing and Implementing Multi-Agent Systems

This section lays the foundation: you'll design a multi-agent system and implement it with CrewAI, integrating LangChain tools for continuity. By the end, your bookstore support team will be up and running, with agents collaborating to solve customer problems.

Designing the System

- **Roles**:

  - **FAQ Agent**: Quick answers from a bookstore FAQ list.

  - **Order Agent**: Checks order status using a mock tool.

  - **Escalation Agent**: Manages urgent or complex issues.

- **Workflow**:

  - User query → FAQ Agent tries first.

  - If unresolved (e.g., "track" or "urgent"), hands off to Order or Escalation Agent.

  - Agents share results back to the user via a lead agent.

- **Goals**:
  - FAQ Agent: Fast, accurate FAQ responses.
  - Order Agent: Precise order updates.
  - Escalation Agent: Swift issue escalation.

Why CrewAI?

CrewAI excels at multi-agent systems:

- Defines agents with roles and goals.
- Manages task delegation and collaboration.
- Integrates with LangChain tools and LLMs. In 2025, it's a top pick for team-based AI, complementing LangChain's single-agent strengths.

Step-by-Step Implementation

Step 1: Set Up Your Environment

1. **Activate Virtual Environment**:
   - cd ai-agent-dev.
   - Windows: venv\Scripts\activate
   - macOS/Linux: source venv/bin/activate.
2. **Create a File**: Make multi_agent_bot.py.

Step 2: Define the Base Setup

- Add:

python

```
from dotenv import load_dotenv

import os

from crewai import Agent, Crew, Task
```

```python
from langchain.llms import OpenAI
from langchain.tools import Tool


load_dotenv()
api_key = os.getenv("OPENAI_API_KEY")
if not api_key:
    raise ValueError("OpenAI API key not found!")
llm = OpenAI(api_key=api_key, temperature=0.7)
```

Step 3: Define Tools (LangChain-Compatible)

- Add:

python

```python
def lookup_book_info(query):
    mock_db = {
        "What's in stock?": " 'The Cosmic Library'  and
'Python Tales'  are in stock.",
        "Any book deals today?": "Buy 2 books, get 10% off
today!"
    }
    return mock_db.get(query, "No info—ask about books!")


def check_order_status(query):
    if "order" in query.lower():
        return "Order #123 is on its way—expect it in 2
days."
```

```
    return "Ask about a book order!"


def escalate_issue(query):

    return f"Escalated '{query}' to bookstore staff-stay
tuned!"


tools = [

    Tool(name="BookLookup", func=lookup_book_info,
description="Find bookstore info."),

    Tool(name="OrderStatus", func=check_order_status,
description="Check book orders."),

    Tool(name="Escalate", func=escalate_issue,
description="Escalate book issues.")
]
```

Step 4: Design Agents with CrewAI

- Add:

python

```python
# FAQ Agent
faq_agent = Agent(

    role="Bookstore FAQ Specialist",

    goal="Answer customer queries using bookstore FAQs
quickly and cheerfully.",

    backstory="You're a book-loving expert who knows the
store's FAQ list inside out.",

    llm=llm,
```

```python
    tools=[tools[0]],  # BookLookup only
    verbose=True
)


# Order Agent
order_agent = Agent(
    role="Order Tracking Specialist",
    goal="Provide accurate order status updates for bookstore customers.",
    backstory="You're a logistics pro, tracking book orders with precision.",
    llm=llm,
    tools=[tools[1]],  # OrderStatus only
    verbose=True
)


# Escalation Agent
escalation_agent = Agent(
    role="Issue Escalation Expert",
    goal="Handle complex or urgent customer issues by escalating them.",
    backstory="You're the calm problem-solver who ensures no reader is left behind.",
    llm=llm,
```

```python
        tools=[tools[2]],  # Escalate only
        verbose=True
)
```

Step 5: Define Tasks and Crew

- Add:

python
```python
def create_tasks(query):
    faq_task = Task(
        description=f"""Answer this query using bookstore
FAQs: {query}
        If it's not an FAQ (e.g., 'track', 'order',
'urgent'), say 'Passing to the right expert!' """,
        agent=faq_agent,
        expected_output="A concise FAQ answer or a handoff
message."
    )
    order_task = Task(
        description=f"Check if this query needs order
tracking: {query}. Use OrderStatus if relevant, else pass it
on.",
        agent=order_agent,
        expected_output="Order status or a handoff message."
    )
    escalation_task = Task(
```

```python
        description=f"Handle this query if it's complex or
urgent: {query}. Escalate if needed, or say 'All set!' ",

        agent=escalation_agent,

        expected_output="Escalation confirmation or closure."

    )

    return [faq_task, order_task, escalation_task]


# Create the crew

def run_multi_agent(query):

    tasks = create_tasks(query)

    crew = Crew(

        agents=[faq_agent, order_agent, escalation_agent],

        tasks=tasks,

        verbose=2  # Detailed logs

    )

    result = crew.kickoff()

    return result
```

Step 6: Add Interactive Loop

- Add:

python

```python
if __name__ == "__main__":

    print("Welcome to the Bookstore Support Team! Type 'quit'
to exit.")

    while True:
```

```
query = input("Your question: ").strip()

if query.lower() == "quit":

    print("Happy reading—bye!")

    break

if not query:

    print("Ask us something bookish!")

    continue

result = run_multi_agent(query)

print(f"Team Response: {result}")
```

Step 7: Test the System

Run: python multi_agent_bot.py

Interact:

Welcome to the Bookstore Support Team! Type 'quit' to exit.

Your question: What's your return policy for books?

Team Response: You can return books within 30 days, unread condition—happy reading!

Your question: Can you track my order?

Team Response: Order #123 is on its way—expect it in 2 days.

Your question: My book is lost—urgent!

Team Response: Escalated 'My book is lost—urgent!' to bookstore staff—stay tuned!

Your question: quit

Happy reading—bye!

How It Works

- **Agents**: Each has a role, goal, and tool—FAQ, Order, Escalation.
- **Tasks**: Define what each agent does with the query.
- **Crew**: Coordinates agents, running tasks sequentially or collaboratively (CrewAI decides based on task outputs).
- **LangChain Tools**: Integrate seamlessly with CrewAI, leveraging Chapter 5's work.

Customizing the System

- **More Agents**: Add a "Recommendations Agent" for book suggestions.
- **Memory**: Integrate LangChain memory per agent (Section 6.2).
- **Logic**: Tweak tasks—e.g., "FAQ Agent retries before handoff."

Troubleshooting

- **No Handoff**: Check task descriptions—explicitly say "pass it on."
- **Errors**: Ensure crewai is installed (pip install crewai).
- **Slow**: Reduce verbose level or agent count.

Why This Matters in 2025

Multi-agent systems like this power complex workflows—think 70% query automation with specialized teams. Your bookstore crew is a microcosm of that, ready to scale.

Next Steps

Section 6.2 adds agent communication and memory for tighter collaboration.

You've designed and built a multi-agent system with CrewAI—FAQ, Order, and Escalation agents working as a team. This isn't just a bot; it's a support squad, echoing 2025's AI trends. Great start—let's make them talk next!

6.2 Communication and Coordination Between Agents

In Section 6.1, you built a multi-agent system with CrewAI where FAQ, Order, and Escalation agents tackled customer queries in a basic sequence. Now, it's time to make them truly collaborative by adding communication and coordination—enabling them to share information, adjust tasks dynamically, and work as a cohesive team. Using CrewAI's task handoff and LangChain's memory, you'll enhance the bookstore support system so agents talk to each other—like passing a query from FAQ to Order with context—mirroring the sophisticated teamwork of 2025's AI-driven support crews. Let's get them chatting and coordinating.

Why Communication and Coordination?

Without interaction, agents operate in silos:

- FAQ Agent might say "I don't know" when Order Agent could help.

- Escalation Agent might repeat work if context isn't shared.

- No memory means no continuity across the team. In 2025, multi-agent systems thrive on collaboration—handling 70% of queries by passing tasks smartly, boosting efficiency by 30%. Here, you'll make that happen.

Goal for This Section

Enhance the system to:

- Enable agents to communicate results and hand off tasks with context.

- Add shared memory so the team recalls past interactions.

- Coordinate responses for a unified user experience.

Prerequisites

- Working system from Section 6.1 (multi_agent_bot.py).

- CrewAI and LangChain installed (pip install crewai langchain langchain-community python-dotenv).

- OpenAI API key in .env.

Step-by-Step Implementation

Step 1: Recap the Base System

Here's the core from Section 6.1:

python

```
from dotenv import load_dotenv

import os

from crewai import Agent, Crew, Task

from langchain.llms import OpenAI

from langchain.tools import Tool


load_dotenv()

api_key = os.getenv("OPENAI_API_KEY")

llm = OpenAI(api_key=api_key, temperature=0.7)


def lookup_book_info(query):

    mock_db = {"What's in stock?": " 'The Cosmic Library'
and 'Python Tales' ."}

    return mock_db.get(query, "No info-ask about books!")


def check_order_status(query):
```

```python
    if "order" in query.lower():

        return "Order #123 is on its way-expect it in 2
days."

    return "Ask about a book order!"


def escalate_issue(query):

    return f"Escalated '{query}' to bookstore staff-stay
tuned!"


tools = [
    Tool(name="BookLookup", func=lookup_book_info,
description="Find bookstore info."),

    Tool(name="OrderStatus", func=check_order_status,
description="Check book orders."),

    Tool(name="Escalate", func=escalate_issue,
description="Escalate book issues.")
]


faq_agent = Agent(role="Bookstore FAQ Specialist",
goal="Answer FAQs", backstory="Book expert.", llm=llm,
tools=[tools[0]], verbose=True)

order_agent = Agent(role="Order Tracking Specialist",
goal="Track orders", backstory="Logistics pro.", llm=llm,
tools=[tools[1]], verbose=True)
```

```python
escalation_agent = Agent(role="Issue Escalation Expert",
goal="Escalate issues", backstory="Problem-solver.", llm=llm,
tools=[tools[2]], verbose=True)


def create_tasks(query):
    faq_task = Task(description=f"Answer FAQ: {query}. If not
FAQ, say 'Passing to expert!' ", agent=faq_agent,
expected_output="FAQ answer or handoff.")

    order_task = Task(description=f"Check order: {query}. Use
OrderStatus if relevant, else pass.", agent=order_agent,
expected_output="Status or handoff.")

    escalation_task = Task(description=f"Escalate if complex:
{query}. Use Escalate if needed.", agent=escalation_agent,
expected_output="Escalation or closure.")

    return [faq_task, order_task, escalation_task]


def run_multi_agent(query):
    tasks = create_tasks(query)

    crew = Crew(agents=[faq_agent, order_agent,
escalation_agent], tasks=tasks, verbose=2)

    return crew.kickoff()


if __name__ == "__main__":
    print("Welcome to the Bookstore Support Team! Type 'quit'
to exit.")

    while True:
```

```python
        query = input("Your question: ").strip()

        if query.lower() == "quit":

            print("Happy reading-bye!")

            break

        if not query:

            print("Ask us something bookish!")

            continue

        result = run_multi_agent(query)

        print(f"Team Response: {result}")
```

Step 2: Add Shared Memory

Integrate LangChain's memory for team context:

- Update imports and setup:

python

```python
from langchain.memory import ConversationBufferMemory


# Shared memory for the crew

memory = ConversationBufferMemory()
```

Step 3: Enhance Agents with Memory and Communication

Add memory and collaboration cues:

- Update agents:

python

```python
faq_agent = Agent(

    role="Bookstore FAQ Specialist",
```

```python
    goal="Answer FAQs and pass unresolved queries to
teammates.",

    backstory="You're a book expert who loves teamwork.",

    llm=llm,

    tools=[tools[0]],

    memory=memory,   # Add memory

    verbose=True

)


order_agent = Agent(

    role="Order Tracking Specialist",

    goal="Track orders using context from teammates.",

    backstory="You're a logistics pro who syncs with the
crew.",

    llm=llm,

    tools=[tools[1]],

    memory=memory,

    verbose=True

)


escalation_agent = Agent(

    role="Issue Escalation Expert",

    goal="Escalate issues with full context from the team.",
```

```
        backstory="You're the calm fixer who ties it all
together.",

        llm=llm,

        tools=[tools[2]],

        memory=memory,

        verbose=True

)
```

Step 4: Update Tasks for Coordination

Make tasks collaborative with context:

- Update create_tasks:

python

```
def create_tasks(query):

    faq_task = Task(

        description=f"""Answer this using FAQs: {query}.

        Use chat history for context.

        If not an FAQ (e.g., 'track', 'order',
'urgent'), say 'Passing to {order_agent.role if "order" in
query.lower() else escalation_agent.role}!' """,

        agent=faq_agent,

        expected_output="FAQ answer or handoff message with
context."

    )

    order_task = Task(

        description=f"""Check if this needs order tracking:
{query}.
```

```python
        Use history and FAQ Agent's input. Use OrderStatus
if relevant, else say 'Passing to
{escalation_agent.role}!' """,

        agent=order_agent,

        expected_output="Order status or handoff."

    )

    escalation_task = Task(

        description=f"""Handle if complex/urgent: {query}.

        Use history and prior agent inputs. Escalate if
needed, else summarize team result.""",

        agent=escalation_agent,

        expected_output="Escalation or final answer."

    )

    return [faq_task, order_task, escalation_task]
```

Step 5: Refine the Crew for Collaboration

Ensure tasks flow and consolidate output:

- Update run_multi_agent:

python

```python
def run_multi_agent(query):

    tasks = create_tasks(query)

    crew = Crew(

        agents=[faq_agent, order_agent, escalation_agent],

        tasks=tasks,

        verbose=2,
```

```
        process="sequential"  # Explicitly sequential for now
    )
    result = crew.kickoff()
    # Consolidate final output (last task's result)
    return result
```

Step 6: Test Coordination and Memory

Run: python multi_agent_bot.py

Interact:

Welcome to the Bookstore Support Team! Type 'quit' to exit.

Your question: How long does shipping take for books?

Team Response: 3-5 business days in the US—your books are on the way!

Your question: Can you track it?

Team Response: Order #123 is on its way—expect it in 2 days.

Your question: It's late—help!

Team Response: Escalated 'It's late—help!' to bookstore staff—stay tuned!

Your question: quit

Happy reading—bye!

Verbose Logs: See handoffs:

[FAQ Agent] Not an FAQ—Passing to Order Tracking Specialist!

[Order Agent] Using OrderStatus—Order #123...

[Escalation Agent] History shows order tracked, now urgent—Escalating!

How It Works

- **Memory**: ConversationBufferMemory shares chat history across agents.

- **Communication**: Tasks include handoff messages (e.g., "Passing to..."), guiding the next agent.

- **Coordination**: CrewAI runs tasks sequentially, but agents use prior outputs and memory to adjust.

- **Output**: Escalation Agent often finalizes, summarizing or escalating.

Customizing Coordination

- **Parallel Tasks**: Set process="parallel" in Crew for simultaneous work (needs careful output merging).

- **More Context**: Add "Share with team: [info]" in task outputs.

- **Memory Type**: Switch to ConversationSummaryMemory for long chats.

Troubleshooting

- **No Handoff**: Check task descriptions—explicitly name the next agent.

- **Memory Missing**: Ensure memory is in each agent's setup.

- **Confused Output**: Simplify tasks or use verbose=1 for clarity.

Why This Matters in 2025

Coordinated multi-agent systems are 2025's backbone—think support teams handling thousands of queries daily. Your bookstore crew shows how specialization and teamwork scale AI impact.

Next Steps

Section 6.3's exercise tests this system with complex scenarios.

You've made your agents talk and coordinate—sharing memory, handing off tasks, and delivering unified answers. This is multi-agent magic, ready for 2025's challenges. Great work—let's test it next!

6.3 Examples of Collaborative Problem-Solving

In Section 6.2, you built a multi-agent system where FAQ, Order, and Escalation agents collaborate using CrewAI, sharing memory and coordinating tasks to handle customer queries. Now, it's time to see this teamwork in action with real-world-inspired examples of collaborative problem-solving. This section walks through three scenarios—each showcasing how your bookstore support team tackles complex, multi-step issues—demonstrating the power of multi-agent systems in 2025. These examples highlight how agents divide labor, communicate, and resolve problems together, paving the way for your own experiments.

Why Collaborative Problem-Solving?

Single agents can falter with intricate tasks—multi-agent systems shine by:

- **Dividing Work**: Each agent focuses on its strength (FAQs, orders, escalation).

- **Sharing Context**: Memory and handoffs ensure seamless teamwork.

- **Solving Complexity**: Combined efforts handle what one can't alone. In 2025, this collaboration drives 70% query automation and 30% productivity gains—your system's a microcosm of that.

Goal for This Section

Explore three examples:

1. A multi-part query needing FAQ and order info.

2. An urgent issue requiring escalation with context.

3. A vague request clarified through teamwork. You'll see how the system from Section 6.2 performs and learn to adapt it.

Prerequisites

- Working system from Section 6.2 (multi_agent_bot.py).

- CrewAI and LangChain installed (pip install crewai langchain langchain-community python-dotenv).

- OpenAI API key in .env.

Example 1: Multi-Part Query

Scenario: "What's your return policy, and can you track my order?"

How It Plays Out

1. **FAQ Agent**:

   o Input: "What's your return policy, and can you track my order?"

   o Reasoning: Recognizes "return policy" as an FAQ, but "track my order" isn't.

   o Action: Answers FAQ part—"Returns within 30 days, unread condition."—then says, "Passing to Order Tracking Specialist for tracking!"

2. **Order Agent**:

   o Input: Query + FAQ Agent's output.

   o Reasoning: Sees "track" and uses OrderStatus tool.

   o Action: "Order #123 is on its way—expect it in 2 days."

3. **Escalation Agent**:

   o Input: Query + prior outputs.

   o Reasoning: No urgency or complexity—teamwork resolved it.

   o Action: Combines: "Returns within 30 days, unread condition. Order #123 is on its way—expect it in 2 days."

Output

Team Response: Returns within 30 days, unread condition. Order #123 is on its way—expect it in 2 days.

Example 2: Urgent Issue with Context

Scenario: User asks, "How long does shipping take?" then "It's late—help now!"

How It Plays Out

1. **First Query: "How long does shipping take?"**

    o **FAQ Agent**: "3-5 business days in the US—your books are on the way!"

    o **Order Agent**: No action needed—passes.

    o **Escalation Agent**: Confirms resolution—"All set!"

    o Output: "3-5 business days in the US—your books are on the way!"

    o Memory: Stores this exchange.

2. **Second Query: "It's late—help now!"**

    o **FAQ Agent**: No FAQ match—"Passing to Issue Escalation Expert!"

    o **Order Agent**: Checks memory—"Shipping was 3-5 days"—but no status update needed, passes.

    o **Escalation Agent**: Sees urgency and prior shipping talk—"Escalated 'It's late—help now!' to bookstore staff—stay tuned!"

Output

First Response: 3-5 business days in the US—your books are on the way!

Second Response: Escalated 'It's late—help now!' to bookstore staff—stay tuned!

Example 3: Vague Request Clarified

Scenario: "I need help with my purchase."

How It Plays Out

1. **FAQ Agent**:
   - Reasoning: Too vague—no FAQ match.
   - Action: "Passing to Order Tracking Specialist to check if it's order-related!"

2. **Order Agent**:
   - Reasoning: "Purchase" could mean order, but needs specifics—tries OrderStatus.
   - Action: "Ask about a book order!"—passes to Escalation.

3. **Escalation Agent**:
   - Reasoning: Still unclear, team can't resolve without more.
   - Action: "Can you tell us more about your purchase? Order issue or something else?"

Output

Team Response: Can you tell us more about your purchase? Order issue or something else?

How It Works with Your Code

Your multi_agent_bot.py from Section 6.2 supports this:

- **Memory**: ConversationBufferMemory tracks history (e.g., shipping → late).

- **Tasks**: Sequential flow—FAQ tries, hands off if needed, Order or Escalation steps in.

- **Coordination**: Task descriptions and agent roles guide handoffs.

- **Output**: CrewAI consolidates results—last agent often finalizes.

Testing These Examples

1. **Run**: python multi_agent_bot.py

2. **Try Them**:

   o "What's your return policy, and can you track my order?"

   o "How long does shipping take?" then "It's late—help now!"

   o "I need help with my purchase."

3. **Check Logs**: verbose=2 shows each agent's reasoning and handoffs.

Enhancing Collaboration

- **Dynamic Handoffs**: Add task dependencies—e.g., Order Agent waits for FAQ output.

python

```
order_task.context = [faq_task]  # In create_tasks
```

- **Better Consolidation**: Make Escalation Agent summarize all outputs explicitly:

python

```
escalation_task.description += " Summarize team efforts if no escalation."
```

- **Memory Tweaks**: Use ConversationSummaryMemory for efficiency:

python

```
from langchain.memory import ConversationSummaryMemory

memory = ConversationSummaryMemory(llm=llm)
```

Troubleshooting

- **Missed Context**: Ensure "history" is in task descriptions.

- **No Collaboration**: Check handoff phrases—e.g., "Passing to…" must match agent roles.

- **Mixed Output**: Adjust Crew to return tasks[-1].output explicitly.

Why This Matters in 2025

These examples show multi-agent systems solving real problems—multi-part queries, urgent escalations, and vague requests—like support teams in top firms. Your bookstore crew is a practical demo of 2025's AI potential.

Next Steps

Section 6.4's exercise lets you build and test your own multi-agent scenarios.

You've seen your agents collaborate—splitting tasks, sharing context, and solving problems as a team. This is 2025-grade AI—smart, coordinated, and ready for the real world. Let's put it to the test next!

6.4 Exercise: Create a Multi-Agent System and Demonstrate Collaboration

This exercise is your chance to flex everything from Chapter 6—designing, implementing, and coordinating a multi-agent system. You'll build a bookstore support team using CrewAI, with agents collaborating to handle customer queries, leveraging shared memory and task handoffs. By the end, you'll demonstrate their teamwork with test scenarios, proving you can craft a 2025-ready system that tackles complex problems collaboratively. This is hands-on proof of your multi-agent mastery—let's get started!

Objectives

- Create a multi-agent system with distinct roles (FAQ, Order, Escalation).

- Implement shared memory and task coordination.

- Demonstrate collaboration with static and live test cases.

- Reflect on performance and potential enhancements.

Prerequisites

- Python 3.12, virtual environment, and dependencies installed (pip install crewai langchain langchain-community python-dotenv).

- OpenAI API key in .env (e.g., OPENAI_API_KEY=sk-abc123...).

- Familiarity with Sections 6.1-6.3.

Step-by-Step Instructions

Part 1: Set Up Your Environment

1. **Activate Virtual Environment**:

   o cd ai-agent-dev (or your folder).

   o Windows: venv\Scripts\activate

   o macOS/Linux: source venv/bin/activate

   o See (venv) in prompt.

2. **Create a File**: Make bookstore_team.py.

Part 2: Build the Multi-Agent System

1. **Imports and Setup**:

   o Add:

python

```
from dotenv import load_dotenv

import os

from crewai import Agent, Crew, Task

from langchain.llms import OpenAI

from langchain.tools import Tool

from langchain.memory import ConversationBufferMemory
```

```python
load_dotenv()

api_key = os.getenv("OPENAI_API_KEY")

if not api_key:

    raise ValueError("OpenAI API key not found!")

llm = OpenAI(api_key=api_key, temperature=0.7)

memory = ConversationBufferMemory()
```

2. **Define Tools**:

   o Add:

python

```python
def lookup_book_info(query):

    mock_db = {

        "What's in stock?": " 'The Cosmic Library'  and 'Python Tales'  are ready to read!",

        "Any book deals today?": "Buy 2 books, get 10% off-stock up!"

    }

    return mock_db.get(query, "No info-ask something bookish!")


def check_order_status(query):

    if "order" in query.lower():

        return "Order #123 is shipping-due in 2 days."

    return "Got an order number? I'll check!"
```

```python
def escalate_issue(query):

    return f"Escalated '{query}' to our book experts-help's
on the way!"


tools = [

    Tool(name="BookLookup", func=lookup_book_info,
description="Find bookstore details."),

    Tool(name="OrderStatus", func=check_order_status,
description="Track book orders."),

    Tool(name="Escalate", func=escalate_issue,
description="Escalate tricky issues.")
]
```

3. **Create Agents**:

   o Add:

python
```python
faq_agent = Agent(

    role="Bookstore FAQ Guru",

    goal="Answer FAQs with a bookish smile.",

    backstory="You live for books and quick answers.",

    llm=llm,

    tools=[tools[0]],

    memory=memory,

    verbose=True

)
```

```python
order_agent = Agent(
    role="Order Tracker",
    goal="Keep customers updated on their book orders.",
    backstory="You're the shipping whisperer of the
bookstore.",
    llm=llm,
    tools=[tools[1]],
    memory=memory,
    verbose=True
)


escalation_agent = Agent(
    role="Escalation Hero",
    goal="Solve tough problems by escalating with context.",
    backstory="You're the team's safety net for tricky
cases.",
    llm=llm,
    tools=[tools[2]],
    memory=memory,
    verbose=True
)
```

4. **Define Tasks**:

- o Add:

python

```python
def create_tasks(query):
    faq_task = Task(
        description=f"""Answer with FAQs: {query}.

        Use history for context. If not an FAQ (e.g.,
'track', 'urgent'), say 'Passing to {order_agent.role if
"order" in query.lower() else escalation_agent.role}!' """,
        agent=faq_agent,
        expected_output="FAQ answer or handoff."
    )

    order_task = Task(
        description=f"""Check order needs: {query}.

        Use history and FAQ input. Use OrderStatus if
relevant, else say 'Passing to
{escalation_agent.role}!' """,
        agent=order_agent,
        expected_output="Order update or handoff."
    )

    escalation_task = Task(
        description=f"""Handle complexity: {query}.

        Use history and team input. Escalate if needed, else
summarize team work.""",
```

```python
        agent=escalation_agent,

        expected_output="Escalation or final answer."
    )

    return [faq_task, order_task, escalation_task]
```

5. **Run the Crew**:

   o Add:

python

```python
def run_multi_agent(query):

    tasks = create_tasks(query)

    crew = Crew(

        agents=[faq_agent, order_agent, escalation_agent],

        tasks=tasks,

        verbose=2,

        process="sequential"
    )

    return crew.kickoff()
```

Part 3: Test Collaboration

1. **Main Block**:

   o Add:

python

```python
if __name__ == "__main__":

    # Static tests

    sample_queries = [
```

```
        "What's your return policy for books?",

        "Can you track my order and tell me about returns?",

        "My order's late—help fast!"

    ]

    print("Static Tests:")

    for query in sample_queries:

        print(f"\nQuery: {query}")

        print(f"Team: {run_multi_agent(query)}")


    # Live mode

    print("\nLive Bookstore Team! Type 'quit' to exit.")

    while True:

        query = input("Your question: ").strip()

        if query.lower() == "quit":

            print("See you in the stacks!")

            break

        if not query:

            print("Team: Got a question? We're here!")

            continue

        print(f"Team: {run_multi_agent(query)}")
```

Part 4: Run and Verify

Execute: python bookstore_team.py

Expected Output:

Static Tests:

Query: What's your return policy for books?

Team: Returns within 30 days, unread condition—keep those pages pristine!

Query: Can you track my order and tell me about returns?

Team: Returns within 30 days, unread condition. Order #123 is shipping—due in 2 days.

Query: My order's late—help fast!

Team: Escalated 'My order's late—help fast!' to our book experts— help's on the way!

Live Bookstore Team! Type 'quit' to exit.

Your question: How long does shipping take?

Team: 3-5 business days in the US—your books are coming!

Your question: Is it on track?

Team: Order #123 is shipping—due in 2 days.

Your question: quit

See you in the stacks!

Part 5: Customize and Reflect

1. **Tweak It**:

- Add an FAQ: "Do you gift-wrap?" → "Yes, free gift-wrapping on request!"

- Add to lookup_book_info: "New releases?" → "Check out 'Moonlit Pages' this week!"

- Change tone: Try "formal" in task descriptions—e.g., "Answer with courtesy."

2. **Test Again**:

   - Static: "Do you gift-wrap?"

   - Live: "How long does shipping take?" then "Is it on track?" (check memory).

3. **Reflect**:

   - Did agents hand off smoothly (e.g., FAQ to Order)?

   - Was memory useful (e.g., context from shipping to tracking)?

   - How's collaboration—clear roles, good output?

   - Ideas: Add a "Recommendation Agent" or parallel tasks?

Troubleshooting

- **No Handoff**: Ensure task descriptions name next agent explicitly.

- **Memory Fail**: Verify memory in each agent and "history" in tasks.

- **Messy Output**: Use verbose=1 or tweak escalation_task to summarize better.

- **Errors**: Reinstall (pip install --upgrade crewai langchain).

What Success Looks Like

- Static tests show collaboration—e.g., FAQ + Order for multi-part queries.

- Live mode uses memory—e.g., links "shipping" to "track."

- Agents coordinate—handoffs are clear, responses unified.

Why This Matters in 2025

This system mirrors 2025's multi-agent reality—teams handling 70% of queries with specialized roles and teamwork. You've built a mini support crew, ready for real-world scale.

You've created a multi-agent bookstore team—collaborating via memory, tools, and tasks. It's not just code; it's a working squad, showcasing 2025's AI potential. Fantastic job—keep exploring what they can do together!

Chapter 7: Integrating with External Services

Welcome to Chapter 7, where your AI agents step out of isolation and into the real world by connecting to external services. In Chapter 6, you built a collaborative multi-agent system for bookstore support, handling queries with teamwork. Now, you'll enhance that system—or a single agent—by integrating it with APIs like Slack (for team communication) and Calendly (for scheduling), turning it into a practical tool that interacts with live systems. This chapter reflects 2025's demand for AI that doesn't just talk but *acts*—bridging the gap between internal logic and external workflows.

Why Integrate with External Services?

Agents that connect to APIs can:

- **Act in Real-Time**: Fetch live data (e.g., order status) or trigger actions (e.g., send a Slack message).

- **Enhance Collaboration**: Link your AI team to human teams or customers.

- **Scale Impact**: Automate tasks across platforms, boosting efficiency by 30%—a 2025 norm. Your bookstore bot will go from mock tools to real integrations, mirroring industry-grade support systems.

What You'll Learn

- **API Connections**: Hook agents to Slack and Calendly (Section 7.1).

- **Tool Creation**: Build LangChain tools for API calls (Section 7.1).

- **Workflows**: Use APIs in single or multi-agent setups (Section 7.2).

- **Exercise**: Test integrations with real scenarios (Section 7.3).

How It Fits the Bookstore Bot

The bot (or team) will:

- **Slack**: Notify staff about escalations—"Order #123 is late!"

- **Calendly**: Schedule a call for complex issues—"Book a slot to discuss your return." This upgrades it from a static helper to a connected assistant.

7.1 Connecting Agents to APIs (e.g., Slack, Calendly)

This section gets your agent talking to Slack and Calendly APIs. You'll use LangChain to create tools for these services, integrating them into a single-agent setup (adaptable to multi-agent later). By the end, your bot will send Slack messages and fetch Calendly links—real-world actions powered by APIs.

Why Slack and Calendly?

- **Slack**: Instant team communication—perfect for escalations.

- **Calendly**: Seamless scheduling—ideal for customer follow-ups. Both are 2025 staples, widely used and API-friendly.

Prerequisites

- Bot from Chapter 5 or 6 (advanced_bot.py or bookstore_team.py).

- LangChain installed (pip install langchain langchain-community python-dotenv).

- Additional packages: pip install slack-sdk requests.

- API Keys:

   o Slack: Bot token (xoxb-...) from Slack App (OAuth & Permissions).

   o Calendly: Personal access token from calendly.com/integrations/api.

Step-by-Step Implementation

Step 1: Set Up Your Environment

1. **Activate Virtual Environment**:

   o cd ai-agent-dev.

   o Windows: venv\Scripts\activate

o macOS/Linux: source venv/bin/activate.

2. **Create a File**: Make api_bot.py.

3. **Update** .env:

4. OPENAI_API_KEY=sk-abc123...

5. SLACK_TOKEN=xoxb-456...

CALENDLY_TOKEN=xyz789...

Step 2: Define Base Setup and Tools

- Add:

python

```python
from dotenv import load_dotenv

import os

from langchain.llms import OpenAI

from langchain.tools import Tool

from langchain.agents import initialize_agent, AgentType

from langchain.memory import ConversationBufferMemory

import requests

from slack_sdk import WebClient


load_dotenv()

api_key = os.getenv("OPENAI_API_KEY")

slack_token = os.getenv("SLACK_TOKEN")

calendly_token = os.getenv("CALENDLY_TOKEN")

if not all([api_key, slack_token, calendly_token]):
```

```python
    raise ValueError("Missing API keys in .env!")


llm = OpenAI(api_key=api_key, temperature=0.7)

memory = ConversationBufferMemory()


# Slack Tool

slack_client = WebClient(token=slack_token)

def send_slack_message(query):

    try:

        slack_client.chat_postMessage(channel="#support",
text=f"Bot Alert: {query}")

        return "Slack message sent to #support!"

    except Exception as e:

        return f"Slack error: {str(e)}"


# Calendly Tool

def get_calendly_link(query):

    headers = {"Authorization": f"Bearer {calendly_token}"}

    url = "https://api.calendly.com/users/me/event_types"

    try:

        response = requests.get(url, headers=headers)

        response.raise_for_status()

        events = response.json()["collection"]
```

```python
        if events:
            return f"Book a call:
{events[0]['scheduling_url']}"
        return "No Calendly events found."
    except Exception as e:
        return f"Calendly error: {str(e)}"


tools = [
    Tool(name="Slack", func=send_slack_message,
description="Send a message to Slack #support."),
    Tool(name="Calendly", func=get_calendly_link,
description="Get a Calendly scheduling link.")
]
```

Step 3: Set Up the Agent

- Add:

python

```python
faqs = {
    "What's your return policy for books?": "Returns within
30 days, unread condition.",
    "How long does shipping take?": "3-5 business days in the
US."
}


agent = initialize_agent(
    tools=tools,
```

```
        llm=llm,

        agent=AgentType.ZERO_SHOT_REACT_DESCRIPTION,

        memory=memory,

        verbose=True

)


def run_agent(query):

    faq_text = "¥n".join([f"Q: {k}¥nA: {v}" for k, v in
faqs.items()])

    input_text = f"""You're a bookstore support bot. Use
these FAQs:

    {faq_text}
```

Use history for context. Query: {query}

Reason step-by-step:

1. If it's an FAQ, answer directly.

2. If it's urgent or complex (e.g., 'late', 'help'), use Slack to notify staff.

3. If it needs a follow-up (e.g., 'call', 'discuss'), use Calendly for a link.

4. Otherwise, say 'I can help—ask me anything!'

Keep it short and friendly."""

return agent.run(input_text)

Step 4: Add Interactive Loop

- Add:

python

```python
if __name__ == "__main__":
    print("Bookstore Bot with APIs! Type 'quit' to exit.")
    while True:
        query = input("Your question: ").strip()
        if query.lower() == "quit":
            print("Happy reading-bye!")
            break
        if not query:
            print("Bot: Ask me something!")
            continue
        print(f"Bot: {run_agent(query)}")
```

Step 5: Test the Integration

Run: python api_bot.py

Interact:

Bookstore Bot with APIs! Type 'quit' to exit.

Your question: What's your return policy for books?

Bot: Returns within 30 days, unread condition.

Your question: My order is late—help!

Bot: Slack message sent to #support!

Your question: Can we discuss my return?

Bot: Book a call: https://calendly.com/your-event-link

Your question: What's the weather?

Bot: I can help—ask me anything!

Your question: quit

Happy reading—bye!

1. **Check Slack**: See "Bot Alert: My order is late—help!" in #support.

2. **Check Calendly**: Link matches your event type (set up in Calendly).

How It Works

- **Slack Tool**: Posts to #support using slack-sdk—real-time staff alerts.

- **Calendly Tool**: Fetches your first event's URL via API—scheduling made easy.

- **Agent**: ReAct reasons—FAQ first, then tools based on keywords (e.g., "late" → Slack).

- **Memory**: Tracks context across queries.

Customizing the Integration

- **More APIs**: Add a shipping API (e.g., Shippo) for tracking.

- **Slack Channels**: Change to #urgent for escalations.

- **Calendly Logic**: Filter events—e.g., "15-min slots only."

Troubleshooting

- **API Errors**: Verify tokens in .env, check Slack/Calendly app perms.

- **No Tool Use**: Tweak prompt—e.g., "Use Slack for 'urgent' explicitly."

- **Rate Limits**: Add delays if hitting API caps (time.sleep(1)).

Why This Matters in 2025

API-connected agents are 2025's norm—acting on live data and workflows, not just mockups. Your bot's now a bridge to real systems, amplifying its utility.

Next Steps

Section 7.2 explores integrating these into multi-agent workflows.

You've wired your agent to Slack and Calendly—real APIs, real actions. This is 2025-grade AI—connected, practical, and ready to scale. Great job—let's expand it next!

7.2 Using Web Scraping or Other Data Retrieval Methods

In Section 7.1, you connected your bookstore bot to Slack and Calendly APIs, enabling it to send messages and schedule calls. Now, you'll expand its capabilities by adding web scraping and other data retrieval methods—tools that let it fetch real-time info from websites (e.g., book prices, store policies) when APIs aren't enough. This section integrates these into your LangChain agent, making it a versatile data-gatherer that reflects 2025's demand for AI that taps into diverse, live sources to solve customer problems.

Why Web Scraping and Data Retrieval?

APIs are great, but:

- **Not Everything Has an API**: Store hours or book reviews might live on web pages.

- **Real-Time Needs**: Scrape current deals or stock from a site.

- **Flexibility**: Combine APIs, scraping, and mock data for broader coverage. In 2025, agents that pull from multiple sources—like web scraping—power 70% query automation by adapting to unstructured data, boosting efficiency.

Goal for This Section

Enhance the bot to:

- Scrape a mock bookstore website for info (e.g., stock status).

- Use a search tool to find external data (e.g., book reviews).

- Integrate these with existing API tools (Slack, Calendly).

Prerequisites

- Bot from Section 7.1 (api_bot.py).

- LangChain and extras installed (pip install langchain langchain-community python-dotenv requests slack-sdk beautifulsoup4).

- API keys in .env (OpenAI, Slack, Calendly).

Step-by-Step Implementation

Step 1: Recap the Base Agent

Here's the core from Section 7.1:

python

```
from dotenv import load_dotenv

import os

from langchain.llms import OpenAI

from langchain.tools import Tool

from langchain.agents import initialize_agent, AgentType

from langchain.memory import ConversationBufferMemory

import requests
```

```python
from slack_sdk import WebClient


load_dotenv()
api_key = os.getenv("OPENAI_API_KEY")
slack_token = os.getenv("SLACK_TOKEN")
calendly_token = os.getenv("CALENDLY_TOKEN")
llm = OpenAI(api_key=api_key, temperature=0.7)
memory = ConversationBufferMemory()


slack_client = WebClient(token=slack_token)
def send_slack_message(query):
    try:
        slack_client.chat_postMessage(channel="#support",
text=f"Bot Alert: {query}")
        return "Slack message sent to #support!"
    except Exception as e:
        return f"Slack error: {str(e)}"


def get_calendly_link(query):
    headers = {"Authorization": f"Bearer {calendly_token}"}
    url = "https://api.calendly.com/users/me/event_types"
    try:
        response = requests.get(url, headers=headers)
```

```python
        events = response.json()["collection"]

        return f"Book a call: {events[0]['scheduling_url']}"
if events else "No events."

    except Exception as e:
        return f"Calendly error: {str(e)}"


faqs = {

    "What's your return policy for books?": "Returns within
30 days, unread condition.",

    "How long does shipping take?": "3-5 business days in the
US."

}


tools = [

    Tool(name="Slack", func=send_slack_message,
description="Send to Slack #support."),

    Tool(name="Calendly", func=get_calendly_link,
description="Get Calendly link.")

]


agent = initialize_agent(tools=tools, llm=llm,
agent=AgentType.ZERO_SHOT_REACT_DESCRIPTION, memory=memory,
verbose=True)


def run_agent(query):
```

```python
    faq_text = "¥n".join([f"Q: {k}¥nA: {v}" for k, v in faqs.items()])

    input_text = f"""You're a bookstore support bot. Use these FAQs:

    {faq_text}


Use history for context. Query: {query}


Reason step-by-step:

1. If it's an FAQ, answer directly.

2. If urgent/complex (e.g., 'late', 'help'), use Slack.

3. If follow-up needed (e.g., 'call'), use Calendly.

4. Otherwise, say 'I can help—ask me anything!'

Keep it short and friendly."""

    return agent.run(input_text)


if __name__ == "__main__":
    print("Bookstore Bot with APIs! Type 'quit' to exit.")
    while True:
        query = input("Your question: ").strip()
        if query.lower() == "quit":
            print("Happy reading—bye!")
            break
        if not query:
            print("Bot: Ask me something!")
```

```python
        continue
    print(f"Bot: {run_agent(query)}")
```

Step 2: Add Web Scraping Tool

Create a mock bookstore page and scrape it:

- Add before tools:

python

```python
from bs4 import BeautifulSoup


# Mock bookstore page (in reality, scrape a live URL)
mock_html = """
<html>
    <body>
        <div id="stock">In Stock: 'The Cosmic Library',
 'Python Tales' </div>
        <div id="deals">Deal: Buy 2 books, get 10% off!</div>
    </body>
</html>
"""


def scrape_bookstore(query):
    try:
        soup = BeautifulSoup(mock_html, "html.parser")
        if "stock" in query.lower():
```

```python
            stock = soup.find(id="stock").text
            return stock if stock else "No stock info."
        elif "deal" in query.lower():
            deals = soup.find(id="deals").text
            return deals if deals else "No deals found."
        return "Try asking about stock or deals!"
    except Exception as e:
        return f"Scraping error: {str(e)}"
```

Step 3: Add a Search Tool

Simulate web search (mocked for simplicity):

- Add:

python

```python
def search_web(query):
    mock_results = {
        "reviews for The Cosmic Library": "4.5 stars— 'A thrilling read!' ",
        "bookstore hours": "Mon–Sat, 9 AM – 6 PM"
    }
    return mock_results.get(query.lower(), "No results—try a specific question!")
```

Step 4: Update Tools List

- Modify tools:

python

```python
tools = [
```

```
Tool(name="Slack", func=send_slack_message,
description="Send to Slack #support."),

    Tool(name="Calendly", func=get_calendly_link,
description="Get Calendly link."),

    Tool(name="ScrapeBookstore", func=scrape_bookstore,
description="Scrape bookstore site for stock or deals."),

    Tool(name="WebSearch", func=search_web,
description="Search web for extra info.")
]
```

Step 5: Enhance the Prompt

Adjust for new tools:

- Update run_agent:

python

```python
def run_agent(query):
    faq_text = "\n".join([f"Q: {k}\nA: {v}" for k, v in
faqs.items()])

    input_text = f"""You're a bookstore support bot. Use
these FAQs:

    {faq_text}
```

Use history for context. Query: {query}

Reason step-by-step:

1. If it's an FAQ, answer directly.

2. If urgent/complex (e.g., 'late', 'help'), use Slack.

3. If follow-up needed (e.g., 'call'), use Calendly.

4. If about stock/deals, use ScrapeBookstore.

5. If external info needed (e.g., 'reviews', 'hours'), use WebSearch.

6. Otherwise, say 'I can help—ask me anything!'

Keep it short and friendly."""

return agent.run(input_text)

Step 6: Test the Enhanced Bot

Run: python api_bot.py

Interact:

Bookstore Bot with APIs! Type 'quit' to exit.

Your question: What's in stock?

Bot: In Stock: 'The Cosmic Library', 'Python Tales'

Your question: Any deals today?

Bot: Deal: Buy 2 books, get 10% off!

Your question: Reviews for The Cosmic Library?

Bot: 4.5 stars—'A thrilling read!'

Your question: My order is late!

Bot: Slack message sent to #support!

Your question: Can we discuss my order?

Bot: Book a call: https://calendly.com/your-event-link

Your question: quit

Happy reading—bye!

How It Works

- **Scraping**: ScrapeBookstore parses mock HTML for stock or deals—replace mock_html with a real URL (e.g., requests.get("http://bookstore.com")) for live use.

- **Search**: WebSearch mocks external lookups—swap with a real API (e.g., Google Search) later.

- **Agent**: ReAct reasons—FAQ first, then tools based on keywords (e.g., "stock" → scraping).

- **Integration**: Works alongside Slack and Calendly, expanding data sources.

Customizing Retrieval

- **Real Scraping**: Use requests.get("http://real-site.com") and adjust soup.find() for actual tags.

- **Search API**: Integrate SerpAPI (pip install google-search-results):

python

```
from serpapi import GoogleSearch

def search_web(query):

    search = GoogleSearch({"q": query, "api_key": "your-serpapi-key"})

    return search.get_dict().get("organic_results",
[{}])[0].get("snippet", "No results.")
```

- **Cache**: Store scraped data in a dict to avoid repeat calls.

Troubleshooting

- **Scraping Fails**: Check HTML structure—mock vs. real differs; handle with try-except.

- **Tool Ignored**: Refine prompt—e.g., "Use ScrapeBookstore for 'stock' explicitly."

- **Legal Note**: Ensure scraping complies with site terms (robots.txt).

Why This Matters in 2025

Web scraping and retrieval make agents data-savvy—fetching live info when APIs fall short, a key trait of 2025's versatile AI systems.

Next Steps

Section 7.3's exercise combines APIs and scraping in a full test.

You've armed your bot with web scraping and search—pulling data from mock pages and beyond. This is 2025-ready AI—connected and resourceful. Nice work—let's test it fully next!

7.3 Securely Handling Credentials and Data

When building and deploying AI agents, safeguarding credentials and sensitive data is as critical as the core functionality. In 2025, robust security practices are not optional—they're essential for maintaining trust, regulatory compliance, and overall system integrity. This section covers the best practices for handling credentials and data securely throughout development, testing, and production stages.

Best Practices for Managing Credentials

- **Environment Variables and .env Files:**
  Store API keys, tokens, and secret configurations outside your source code. Use environment variables and tools like python-dotenv to load them from a `.env` file that is added to `.gitignore`. This minimizes the risk of accidental exposure when sharing or deploying your code.
- **Secret Management Services:**
  Leverage dedicated secret management tools (e.g., AWS Secrets Manager, Azure Key Vault, HashiCorp Vault) to store and manage credentials securely. These services offer encryption at rest and in transit, access control, and automatic key rotation.

- **Principle of Least Privilege:**
  Ensure that your credentials only have the permissions they need. For instance, if your AI agent only reads data from an API, use a read-only API key. This limits potential damage if a key is compromised.
- **Regular Rotation and Revocation:**
  Implement a key rotation strategy to regularly update credentials. This practice helps reduce the risk window if a key is leaked. Automated rotation can often be configured within your secret management service.

Securing Data in Transit and at Rest

- **Encryption:**
  Use HTTPS for all external API calls to protect data in transit. For sensitive data stored locally or in cloud storage, ensure that encryption is enabled (e.g., using AES-256).
- **Access Control:**
  Implement robust access control mechanisms. Use multi-factor authentication (MFA) for accessing your development environments and production systems. Limit access to sensitive data to only those roles or services that require it.
- **Data Masking and Anonymization:**
  When dealing with user data, consider techniques like data masking or anonymization to protect personally identifiable information (PII) during testing or analysis.

Secure Coding Practices

- **Avoid Hardcoding Secrets:**
  Never embed credentials directly in your source code. Instead, retrieve them from secure sources at runtime.
- **Audit and Logging:**
  Regularly audit your codebase and configuration files for any accidental exposure of sensitive data. Implement logging mechanisms that do not log sensitive information.
- **Dependency Management:**
  Keep all libraries and dependencies up-to-date, as outdated packages may contain vulnerabilities. Use tools like pip-audit to scan for known issues in your dependencies.

Integrating Security into Your AI Agent Workflow

When integrating external services such as Slack or Calendly, ensure that your API keys and tokens are handled securely throughout the lifecycle:

- **During Development:**
  Use .env files for local testing and ensure these files are excluded from version control. Test your integrations in isolated environments.
- **In Production:**
  Deploy your agent within secure infrastructure, using managed secret services and strict network policies. Monitor access logs and set up alerts for suspicious activities.

Exercise: Implement and Test Secure Credential Management

Objectives:

- Refactor your project to use environment variables for all credentials.
- Set up a local secret management simulation using a .env file.
- Verify that no sensitive data is present in your code repository.
- Test the agent's integration with an external service (e.g., Slack) to ensure secure transmission of credentials.

Steps:

1. **Create a .env File:**
   Include entries such as:

   ```plaintext
   OPENAI_API_KEY=sk-abc123...
   SLACK_TOKEN=xoxb-456...
   CALENDLY_TOKEN=xyz789...
   ```

2. **Load Credentials Securely:**
   In your Python scripts, use:

   ```python
   from dotenv import load_dotenv
   import os
   ```

```
load_dotenv()
api_key = os.getenv("OPENAI_API_KEY")
slack_token = os.getenv("SLACK_TOKEN")
calendly_token = os.getenv("CALENDLY_TOKEN")
```

3. **Verify Exclusion:**
   Ensure your `.env` file is added to `.gitignore` to prevent accidental commits.
4. **Simulate Access:**
   Write a small script that uses these credentials to make a simple API call (e.g., post a test message to Slack) and confirm that it executes without exposing sensitive details.
5. **Review and Audit:**
   Use tools like GitGuardian or manual code reviews to audit your repository for any hardcoded secrets.

By following these guidelines, you not only protect your project and data but also align your development practices with the industry standards expected in 2025. Secure handling of credentials and data is a foundation upon which robust, trustworthy AI agents are built.

Exercise 7.4: Integrate Your Agent with an External Service and Handle Secure Data

In this hands-on exercise, you will integrate your AI agent with an external service **(e.g., OpenAI, Slack, Twilio, or Google Sheets)** while following best security practices for handling sensitive data, such as API keys and user inputs.

Objective

1. **Connect an AI agent to an external API** (e.g., Slack for messaging, Twilio for SMS, or Google Sheets for logging responses).
2. **Securely manage API credentials** using environment variables.
3. **Encrypt sensitive data** before storing it.
4. **Log and monitor API usage** while avoiding exposure of sensitive data.

Step 1: Choose an External Service

For this exercise, we will integrate an AI-powered assistant with **Slack**, allowing it to send messages securely.

- **Why Slack?** It's widely used for communication and has a well-documented API.
- **Alternatives:** If you prefer, you can integrate with **Google Sheets (to store data), Twilio (to send SMS), or OpenAI API (to process text queries).**

Step 2: Set Up API Access (Slack)

1. **Create a Slack App**
   - Visit the Slack API dashboard and create a new app.
   - Select "From Scratch" and choose a workspace.
   - Enable the **Bot Token Scope** for `chat:write` (to send messages).
   - Install the app to your workspace and get the **Bot User OAuth Token**.
2. **Store Your API Key Securely**
   - Never hard-code API keys in your code.
   - Use environment variables to store sensitive information. Example:

   ```bash
   export SLACK_BOT_TOKEN="xoxb-your-bot-token"
   ```

   - Use a **secrets manager** in production (e.g., AWS Secrets Manager, HashiCorp Vault).

Step 3: Secure Data Handling

1. **Encrypt sensitive data** before storing it in databases or logs.
2. **Use HTTPS** for API communication to prevent interception.
3. **Log activity safely**, but avoid logging sensitive data.

Step 4: Write Secure Code

Here's a Python script to send a message to Slack while handling secrets securely.

Python Implementation

```python
python

import os
import json
import logging
import requests
from cryptography.fernet import Fernet

# Setup logging (avoid logging sensitive data)
logging.basicConfig(level=logging.INFO)
logger = logging.getLogger(__name__)

# Load API key securely
SLACK_BOT_TOKEN = os.getenv("SLACK_BOT_TOKEN")
if not SLACK_BOT_TOKEN:
    raise EnvironmentError("SLACK_BOT_TOKEN not
found in environment variables.")

# Define the Slack channel
CHANNEL_ID = "C12345678"  # Replace with your
channel ID

# Define encryption key (in practice, store
securely)
ENCRYPTION_KEY = os.getenv("ENCRYPTION_KEY",
Fernet.generate_key())
cipher_suite = Fernet(ENCRYPTION_KEY)

def send_secure_message(message):
    """
    Sends an encrypted message to Slack securely.
    """
```

```python
    encrypted_message =
cipher_suite.encrypt(message.encode())

    url = "https://slack.com/api/chat.postMessage"
    headers = {
        "Authorization": f"Bearer
{SLACK_BOT_TOKEN}",
        "Content-Type": "application/json"
    }
    payload = {
        "channel": CHANNEL_ID,
        "text": f"Encrypted Message:
{encrypted_message.decode()}"
    }

    response = requests.post(url, headers=headers,
data=json.dumps(payload))

    if response.status_code == 200:
        logger.info("Message sent successfully.")
    else:
        logger.error(f"Error sending message:
{response.text}")

# Send an encrypted message
send_secure_message("Hello, this is a secure AI
message!")
```

Step 5: Test and Monitor

1. **Run the script** and check if the message appears in Slack.
2. **Monitor API usage** to detect unusual activity.
3. **Ensure error handling** by testing invalid API keys.

Bonus: Extend This Exercise

- Integrate with **Google Sheets** for logging messages securely.
- Use **Twilio API** to send SMS alerts while encrypting user data.
- Implement **role-based access control (RBAC)** to restrict API usage.

You successfully integrated your AI agent with an external service while applying security best practices.
This ensures **API security, data encryption, and secure logging**, making your AI integrations safe and reliable.

Chapter 8: Training and Optimizing AI Agents

8.1 Training Techniques

Training AI agents effectively is crucial to improving their decision-making, adaptability, and efficiency in dynamic environments. This chapter explores **different training techniques**, with a focus on **reinforcement learning (RL)** and other methods used for optimizing AI agent performance.

---

1. Understanding Training for AI Agents

AI agents are trained using **various learning paradigms** depending on their function:

- **Supervised Learning** (labeled datasets for classification or regression tasks)
- **Unsupervised Learning** (clustering, anomaly detection, etc.)
- **Reinforcement Learning (RL)** (learning from rewards in an environment)
- **Imitation Learning** (mimicking expert demonstrations)
- **Self-Supervised Learning** (predicting parts of input data)

For **autonomous AI agents, reinforcement learning** is a key approach.

---

2. Reinforcement Learning (RL) for AI Agents

2.1 What is Reinforcement Learning?

Reinforcement Learning (RL) is a **trial-and-error-based** learning approach where an agent interacts with an environment and **learns from rewards and penalties** to optimize its actions.

- **Agent**: The AI system making decisions
- **Environment**: The world where the agent operates
- **Actions (A)**: Choices the agent can make
- **State (S)**: The current situation of the agent in the environment
- **Reward (R)**: Feedback for an action (positive or negative)

The goal of RL is to **maximize cumulative rewards over time**.

2.2 Key RL Algorithms

1. Q-Learning (Model-Free RL)

A popular algorithm where an agent learns an optimal action-selection policy using a **Q-table**.

- **Formula:**

  $$Q(s,a) = Q(s,a) + \alpha\,[r + \gamma \max Q(s',a') - Q(s,a)]$$

  where:

    - $Q(s,a)$ = Expected future reward of an action a in state s
    - α = Learning rate
    - γ = Discount factor (importance of future rewards)
    - r = Immediate reward
    - s', a' = Next state and next action

Best for discrete action spaces

---

2. Deep Q-Networks (DQN)

Uses **deep neural networks** instead of Q-tables for **large and complex environments**.

Best for complex, high-dimensional spaces (e.g., video games, robotics).

---

3. Policy Gradient Methods

Instead of learning a Q-value for state-action pairs, these methods **learn a policy directly**.

- **REINFORCE Algorithm**: Uses Monte Carlo estimates for training policies.
- **Actor-Critic Methods**: Combines value-based (critic) and policy-based (actor) learning.

Best for continuous action spaces and real-time decision-making.

---

4. Proximal Policy Optimization (PPO)

A modern RL algorithm used in **OpenAI's GPT training** that stabilizes policy updates and prevents performance degradation.

Used in robotics, NLP, and gaming AI.

2.3 Implementing RL for AI Agents

Step 1: Install Dependencies

```bash
pip install gym numpy torch stable-baselines3
```

Step 2: Define an RL Agent Using Stable-Baselines3

```python
import gym
from stable_baselines3 import PPO

# Create environment
env = gym.make("CartPole-v1")

# Initialize RL agent with PPO
model = PPO("MlpPolicy", env, verbose=1)

# Train the agent
model.learn(total_timesteps=10000)
```

```
# Save the trained model
model.save("ppo_cartpole")

# Test the trained model
obs = env.reset()
for _ in range(1000):
    action, _states = model.predict(obs)
    obs, reward, done, info = env.step(action)
    env.render()
    if done:
        obs = env.reset()
env.close()
```

3. Alternative Training Techniques

3.1 Imitation Learning

Instead of trial-and-error, an AI agent **learns by mimicking human demonstrations**.

- **Behavior Cloning** (Supervised Learning from expert actions)
- **Generative Adversarial Imitation Learning (GAIL)**

Used in self-driving cars, robotics, and AI assistants.

3.2 Self-Supervised Learning for AI Agents

- AI learns **patterns from unlabeled data** by creating its own training labels.
- Used in **LLMs (e.g., GPT-4) and autonomous agents**.

Best for language models, vision, and self-learning agents.

4. Optimizing AI Agents

Once an agent is trained, optimization techniques improve its performance:

4.1 Hyperparameter Tuning

- **Learning Rate**: Determines how fast the model updates.
- **Discount Factor (γ)**: Defines how much future rewards matter.
- **Exploration vs. Exploitation**: Balancing trying new actions vs. using known ones.

Use grid search or Bayesian optimization to find the best settings.

4.2 Transfer Learning for AI Agents

- Apply a **pre-trained AI model** to a new environment with minor fine-tuning.
- **Example**: Use an RL-trained AI in **one game** and adapt it to another.

Speeds up training for real-world applications.

4.3 Continuous Learning & Adaptation

- **Retraining** on new experiences improves adaptability.
- Use **meta-learning** for AI agents to self-adjust in real time.

Best for changing environments like finance, robotics, and chatbots.

Training AI agents involves **reinforcement learning, imitation learning, and self-supervised methods**. Optimizing them requires **hyperparameter tuning, transfer learning, and continuous adaptation**.

8.2 Evaluating Agent Performance

Evaluating the performance of AI agents is crucial to ensuring they operate effectively, make optimal decisions, and continuously improve over time. This section covers different **evaluation techniques, key performance metrics, benchmarking methods, and real-world testing strategies** for assessing agent performance.

1. Why Evaluating AI Agents is Important

Before deploying an AI agent in a real-world environment, we need to:
Measure accuracy and reliability
Ensure adaptability to dynamic environments
Optimize efficiency and resource utilization
Detect and correct biases or failures

A well-evaluated agent is **more robust, trustworthy, and scalable**.

2. Key Metrics for Evaluating AI Agents

Depending on the agent's purpose, we use different evaluation criteria. Here are the most important ones:

2.1 Task-Specific Performance Metrics

- **Accuracy**: How often the agent makes the correct decision.
- **Success Rate**: Percentage of tasks successfully completed.
- **Precision & Recall**: Important for classification-based AI agents.

2.2 Reinforcement Learning (RL) Metrics

For RL agents, we focus on:

- **Cumulative Reward**: Sum of all rewards over time.
- **Convergence Speed**: How fast the agent learns an optimal policy.
- **Exploration vs. Exploitation Balance**: Ensuring the agent explores new strategies instead of sticking to suboptimal ones.

2.3 Efficiency and Computational Cost

- **Inference Time**: How fast the agent makes a decision.
- **Memory Usage**: How much system memory the agent consumes.
- **Scalability**: How well the agent performs with more data or users.

2.4 Robustness and Adaptability

- **Error Recovery Rate**: How well the agent corrects its mistakes.
- **Generalization**: Can the agent perform well on unseen data?
- **Stress Testing**: Evaluating performance under extreme conditions.

---

3. Methods for Evaluating AI Agents

3.1 Offline Evaluation (Pre-Deployment)

Before deploying, we test the agent in controlled environments:

- **Simulations**: Test in virtual environments (e.g., OpenAI Gym, Unity ML-Agents).
- **Historical Data Replay**: Use past real-world data to assess agent performance.

Example: Evaluating a self-driving AI
Simulate different traffic conditions before deploying in real streets.

3.2 Online Evaluation (Live Testing)

Once deployed, we monitor real-world interactions:

- **A/B Testing**: Compare different versions of the agent.
- **User Feedback & Ratings**: Gather human evaluations.
- **Error Logs & Failures**: Track where and why the agent fails.

Example: Evaluating a Chatbot
Deploy different chatbot models and measure user satisfaction.

---

4. Benchmarking AI Agents

To compare an AI agent's performance, we use **benchmarking frameworks**:

- **OpenAI Gym**: Standard RL environments.
- **SuperGLUE & GLUE**: For NLP model performance.

- **MLPerf**: Industry-standard AI model benchmarking.

Example: Comparing AI Trading Bots
Test different trading bots on historical stock market data and compare profit margins.

---

5. Automating Agent Evaluation

Automating the evaluation process saves time and ensures continuous monitoring.
. **Use MLOps tools** like:

- **TensorBoard**: Visualize training metrics.
- **Prometheus & Grafana**: Monitor real-time AI performance.
- **Weights & Biases (WandB)**: Track AI experiments.

Code Example: Logging Agent Performance with Weights & Biases

```python
import wandb

wandb.init(project="ai-agent-evaluation")

# Log evaluation metrics
wandb.log({"success_rate": 0.92, "response_time": 0.5,
"error_rate": 0.03})
```

---

6. Improving AI Agent Performance Based on Evaluation

After evaluating, apply **optimizations** to improve the agent:

1☐. **Adjust hyperparameters** (learning rate, batch size, etc.).
2☐. **Retrain with better datasets** to reduce bias.
3☐. **Fine-tune models** using transfer learning or additional training.
4☐. **Implement feedback loops** to adapt over time.

Example: Enhancing a Speech Recognition AI
If evaluation shows **high error rates in noisy environments**, retrain the model using audio samples with background noise.

Evaluating AI agents involves **measuring performance, benchmarking, and automating monitoring**. Regular evaluations help **fine-tune AI agents, enhance their decision-making capabilities, and ensure robustness** in real-world applications.

8.3 Optimizing Agent Behavior for Specific Tasks

Optimizing an AI agent for specific tasks ensures **better accuracy, efficiency, and adaptability**. Whether the agent is a **chatbot, a recommendation system, a trading bot, or an autonomous robot**, the optimization process follows structured techniques.

---

1. Why Optimize AI Agents?

An optimized agent: Performs tasks **faster and more accurately**
Reduces **resource consumption**
Adapts to **real-world challenges**
Provides **better user experiences**

Example: A customer support chatbot should **quickly retrieve accurate answers** while minimizing unnecessary API calls.

---

2. Strategies for Optimizing AI Agents

2.1 Task-Specific Fine-Tuning

Adjusting the AI model based on domain-specific data improves performance.

Example: Optimizing a Chatbot for Legal Advice

- Instead of general training, fine-tune the chatbot using **legal case studies, regulations, and legal terminology**.
- Use **Transfer Learning** from a general NLP model to a legal dataset.

Code Example: Fine-tuning an LLM for legal support

python

```
from transformers import AutoModelForCausalLM, AutoTokenizer


model_name = "meta-llama/Meta-Llama-3-8B"

model = AutoModelForCausalLM.from_pretrained(model_name)

tokenizer = AutoTokenizer.from_pretrained(model_name)


# Fine-tune on legal data

legal_text = "In accordance with section 42 of the legal code..."

inputs = tokenizer(legal_text, return_tensors="pt")

outputs = model(**inputs)
```

2.2 Reinforcement Learning for Task Optimization

Agents that **learn through rewards** (Reinforcement Learning - RL) can optimize themselves over time.

Example: Training a Robot to Pick Objects

- Use **Reinforcement Learning (RL)** to reward successful object pickups.
- Adjust movement based on failures and successes.

Code Example: RL-based Optimization Using OpenAI Gym

```python
import gym

env = gym.make("CartPole-v1")  # Example RL environment
state = env.reset()

for _ in range(1000):
    action = env.action_space.sample()  # Select an action
    state, reward, done, _ = env.step(action)  # Apply action
    if done:
        state = env.reset()
```

2.3 Hyperparameter Tuning

Selecting the best **learning rate, batch size, and network architecture** improves model efficiency.

Example: Optimizing a Fraud Detection Agent

- Adjust **learning rate** for better training stability.
- Use **grid search** or **Bayesian optimization** to find optimal parameters.

Code Example: Hyperparameter Tuning Using Optuna

```python
import optuna

def objective(trial):
    learning_rate = trial.suggest_loguniform("learning_rate", 1e-5, 1e-1)
    batch_size = trial.suggest_categorical("batch_size", [16, 32, 64])
    return train_model(learning_rate, batch_size)  # Function to train the agent

study = optuna.create_study(direction="maximize")
study.optimize(objective, n_trials=50)
```

2.4 Memory and Computation Optimization

Reducing resource usage is crucial for real-time and embedded AI systems.

Example: Optimizing an Edge AI Model for Mobile Phones

- **Prune the model** (remove unnecessary layers).
- **Use quantization** (reduce precision of weights).
- **Convert to a lightweight format like TensorRT or ONNX.**

Code Example: Converting an AI Model for Efficient Inference

```python
import torch
```

```python
import torch.quantization


model = torch.load("model.pth")
quantized_model = torch.quantization.quantize_dynamic(
    model, {torch.nn.Linear}, dtype=torch.qint8
)
torch.save(quantized_model, "optimized_model.pth")
```

2.5 Adaptability Through Continual Learning

For agents in dynamic environments, **online learning** helps them adapt.

Example: AI Customer Support Bot that Adapts Over Time

- If new FAQs emerge, **incrementally update** the chatbot model.
- Use **feedback loops** to improve responses.

Code Example: Continual Learning with Incremental Data

python

```python
from sklearn.linear_model import SGDClassifier


clf = SGDClassifier()
clf.partial_fit(new_data, new_labels, classes=[0, 1])  #
Train on new customer queries
```

---

3. Case Studies: Optimized Agents in Action

◆ Optimizing a Self-Driving Car Agent

Before Optimization:

- Struggled in foggy weather.
- Took too long to detect pedestrians.

After Optimization: Trained on foggy dataset → Better recognition in bad weather.
Reduced sensor processing time → Faster decisions.

◆ **Optimizing a Recommendation System**

Before Optimization:

- Suggested generic products to users.

After Optimization: Used **personalized embeddings** for better recommendations.
Implemented **real-time updates** based on user interactions.

4.

Optimizing agent behavior involves:

1 □.**Fine-tuning with domain-specific data**
2 □. **Applying Reinforcement Learning for adaptability**
3 □. **Tuning hyperparameters for efficiency**
4 □. **Reducing computational overhead**
5 □. **Using continual learning for real-world adaptation**

8.4 Exercise: Train and Optimize Your Agent for a Specific Task, Evaluate Results

Objective

In this exercise, you will train an AI agent for a specific task, optimize its performance, and evaluate the results. You can choose from various applications, such as a chatbot, image classifier, trading bot, or reinforcement learning agent.

Steps to Complete This Exercise

1 □. Select a task for your agent.
2□. Train the agent using a dataset or an environment.
3□. Optimize the agent using fine-tuning, hyperparameter tuning, or reinforcement learning.
4□. Evaluate the agent's performance using appropriate metrics.
5□. Document the improvements and compare results.

Step 1: Choose a Task

Select a task that your agent will perform. Here are some example tasks:

- **Chatbot:** Answer customer queries.
- **Image Classification:** Identify handwritten digits.
- **Trading Bot:** Predict stock price movements.
- **Reinforcement Learning Agent:** Play a game like CartPole.

 For this exercise, let's optimize an NLP agent (Chatbot) for sentiment analysis.
We will train the agent to classify text as **positive, neutral, or negative** and optimize it for better accuracy.

Step 2: Train the Agent

We use a pre-trained language model (BERT) and fine-tune it on a sentiment analysis dataset.

Install Dependencies

```bash

pip install transformers datasets torch scikit-learn
```

Load and Preprocess the Dataset

```python
python

from datasets import load_dataset
from transformers import AutoTokenizer


# Load sentiment dataset
dataset = load_dataset("imdb")


# Initialize tokenizer
tokenizer = AutoTokenizer.from_pretrained("distilbert-base-uncased")


# Tokenize dataset
def tokenize_function(examples):
    return tokenizer(examples["text"], padding="max_length", truncation=True)


tokenized_datasets = dataset.map(tokenize_function, batched=True)
```

Train a Sentiment Analysis Model

```python
python

from transformers import AutoModelForSequenceClassification, Trainer, TrainingArguments
```

```python
# Load pre-trained model for classification
model =
AutoModelForSequenceClassification.from_pretrained("distilber
t-base-uncased", num_labels=2)


# Set up training arguments
training_args = TrainingArguments(
    output_dir="./results",
    evaluation_strategy="epoch",
    save_strategy="epoch",
    learning_rate=2e-5,
    per_device_train_batch_size=16,
    per_device_eval_batch_size=16,
    num_train_epochs=3,
    weight_decay=0.01,
)


trainer = Trainer(
    model=model,
    args=training_args,
    train_dataset=tokenized_datasets["train"],
    eval_dataset=tokenized_datasets["test"],
```

```
)
```

```
# Train the model

trainer.train()
```

Step 3: Optimize the Agent

Optimization strategies include: **Fine-tuning with more domain-specific data**
Hyperparameter tuning (learning rate, batch size, epochs)
Using smaller/lighter models for speed optimization
Adding more training data for better generalization

Hyperparameter Tuning Using Optuna

python

```python
import optuna


def objective(trial):

    learning_rate = trial.suggest_loguniform("learning_rate",
1e-5, 5e-5)

    batch_size = trial.suggest_categorical("batch_size", [8,
16, 32])


    training_args = TrainingArguments(

        output_dir="./results",

        evaluation_strategy="epoch",

        save_strategy="epoch",
```

```python
        learning_rate=learning_rate,

        per_device_train_batch_size=batch_size,

        num_train_epochs=3,

        weight_decay=0.01,

    )


    trainer = Trainer(

        model=model,

        args=training_args,

        train_dataset=tokenized_datasets["train"],

        eval_dataset=tokenized_datasets["test"],

    )


    result = trainer.train()

    return result.training_loss


study = optuna.create_study(direction="minimize")

study.optimize(objective, n_trials=10)


best_params = study.best_params

print(f"Best Learning Rate: {best_params['learning_rate']},
Best Batch Size: {best_params['batch_size']}")
```

Step 4: Evaluate the Agent

We evaluate using **accuracy, precision, recall, and F1-score**.

Evaluate Model Performance

```python
python

from sklearn.metrics import accuracy_score,
classification_report

import torch


def evaluate_model(model, dataset):
    predictions, labels = [], []
    for batch in dataset:
        inputs = tokenizer(batch["text"],
return_tensors="pt", padding=True, truncation=True)
        outputs = model(**inputs)
        logits = outputs.logits
        preds = torch.argmax(logits, dim=-1)
        predictions.extend(preds.numpy())
        labels.extend(batch["label"])
    return accuracy_score(labels, predictions),
classification_report(labels, predictions)


accuracy, report = evaluate_model(model,
tokenized_datasets["test"])
```

```
print(f"Accuracy: {accuracy}")

print(report)
```

Step 5: Compare Results and Document Improvements

After optimization, compare the performance before and after tuning.
You should see an improvement in:

- **Higher accuracy**
- **Lower loss**
- **Faster inference time** (if using optimizations like quantization)

Challenge Yourself!

1 ⬜Modify the training pipeline for a **different task** (e.g., a chatbot).
2 ⬜Apply **different optimization techniques** (pruning, knowledge
distillation).
3 ⬜Train your agent **on a custom dataset** instead of a pre-existing one.

◆ **Next Step:** Deploy your trained agent for real-world use!

Chapter 9: Testing and Debugging AI Agents

9.1 Strategies for Testing Agent Functionality

Testing AI agents requires a structured approach to ensure reliability, accuracy, and performance across various environments. Unlike traditional software testing, AI agent testing must account for probabilistic behavior, external dependencies, and dynamic interactions. This section explores key strategies to effectively test agent functionality.

1□. Unit Testing for Individual Components

Unit testing ensures that each function or module in your AI agent works correctly in isolation.

Best Practices:

Test core logic functions (e.g., response generation, decision-making).
Mock external dependencies (APIs, databases) to isolate tests.
Use Python testing frameworks like `pytest` or `unittest`.

Example: Unit Testing an AI Agent's Response

`python`

```
import pytest

from my_ai_agent import generate_response


def test_generate_response():

    response = generate_response("Hello!")

    assert isinstance(response, str), "Response should be a
string"
```

```
    assert len(response) > 0, "Response should not be empty"


if __name__ == "__main__":

    pytest.main()
```

2⬜. Integration Testing for Agent Interactions

Integration testing ensures that different components of your AI agent (such as external APIs, databases, or user interfaces) work together seamlessly.

Best Practices:

Test interactions between the agent and APIs.
Simulate real-world data inputs.
Verify system responses against expected outputs.

Example: Testing API Integration with Mocking

python

```
from unittest.mock import MagicMock

from my_ai_agent import fetch_external_data


def test_fetch_external_data():

    mock_api = MagicMock(return_value={"data": "Test
Response"})

    response = fetch_external_data(mock_api)

    assert response["data"] == "Test Response"
```

```
test_fetch_external_data()
```

3□. Functional Testing for End-to-End Workflows

Functional testing ensures the AI agent meets user expectations by testing entire workflows.

Best Practices:

Test scenarios covering different user interactions.
Validate agent outputs against expected business logic.
Use automation tools for large-scale testing.

Example: Automated Functional Testing

```python
python
```

```python
def test_full_workflow():

    user_input = "Find me the nearest restaurant."

    response = my_ai_agent(user_input)

    assert "restaurant" in response.lower(), "Expected a
restaurant suggestion"
```

```
test_full_workflow()
```

4□. Performance and Load Testing

Performance testing evaluates how the AI agent handles different loads, while load testing checks its behavior under stress.

Best Practices:

Measure response times and system latency.
Simulate multiple concurrent users.
Identify bottlenecks using tools like **Locust** or **JMeter**.

Example: Load Testing with Locust

```python
from locust import HttpUser, task


class AIUser(HttpUser):
    @task
    def test_agent_response(self):
        self.client.post("/agent", json={"message":
"Hello!"})


if __name__ == "__main__":
    import os
    os.system("locust -f this_script.py")
```

5□. Regression Testing for Consistency

Regression testing ensures new updates don't break existing
functionality.

Best Practices:

Maintain a baseline dataset for testing old and new versions.
Use automated tests before deploying updates.
Compare model outputs pre- and post-update.

Example: Comparing Outputs for Regression Testing

```python
python

previous_version_output = "The capital of France is Paris."

new_version_output = ai_agent("What is the capital of
France?")

assert previous_version_output == new_version_output,
"Regression detected!"
```

6️⃣.Bias and Fairness Testing

AI agents must be tested for bias to ensure fair decision-making.

Best Practices:

Check responses across diverse demographic inputs.
Use bias detection frameworks like **Fairness Indicators** or **AIF360**.
Analyze model predictions for consistency.

Example: Bias Testing with AIF360

```python
python

from aif360.datasets import AdultDataset

from aif360.metrics import BinaryLabelDatasetMetric


dataset = AdultDataset()

metric = BinaryLabelDatasetMetric(dataset)

print(f"Disparate impact: {metric.disparate_impact()}")
```

7️⃣Security Testing for AI Agents

AI agents interact with sensitive data, making security testing critical.

Best Practices:

Prevent injection attacks in user inputs.
Secure API keys and credentials.
Test for adversarial attacks.

Example: Detecting Injection Attacks

```python
python
```

```python
def test_injection_attack():

    malicious_input = "' OR '1'='1"

    response = my_ai_agent(malicious_input)

    assert "error" in response.lower(), "Injection attack not
detected!"



test_injection_attack()
```

Testing AI agents requires a multi-layered approach, including unit, integration, functional, performance, and security testing. By implementing these strategies, you can ensure your AI agent is **reliable, robust, and fair** in real-world applications.

 Next Section: Debugging AI agents—how to identify and fix issues effectively!

9.2 Debugging Techniques for Common Issues in AI Agents

Debugging AI agents can be challenging due to their probabilistic behavior, complex dependencies, and evolving decision-making processes. This section outlines key debugging techniques to identify and resolve common issues in AI agents.

1□. Debugging Incorrect or Unexpected Outputs

Common Causes:

- **Poor training data**: The model was trained on low-quality or biased data.
- **Incorrect prompt engineering**: The input prompts are ambiguous or unclear.
- **Logic errors in decision-making**: The agent is making faulty inferences.

Debugging Steps:

Log input/output pairs: Track what input the agent received and what output it generated.
Use assertion statements: Ensure the output follows expected rules.
Check embeddings/similarity scores: If the agent uses vector search, verify the retrieved results.

Example: Debugging Output Issues

python

```python
import logging

logging.basicConfig(level=logging.INFO)


def generate_response(input_text):

    response = my_ai_agent(input_text)

    logging.info(f"User Input: {input_text} | Agent Response: {response}")

    return response
```

```python
# Test with different inputs

print(generate_response("What is the capital of France?"))
```

2□. Fixing API Integration Issues

Common Causes:

- **Incorrect API endpoints or parameters**
- **Rate limits from external services**
- **Authentication errors (invalid API keys, expired tokens)**

Debugging Steps:

Print API error messages to understand the failure reason.
Use a mock API for testing before calling a real API.
Check API rate limits and implement retries with exponential backoff.

Example: Handling API Errors Gracefully

python

```python
import requests


def fetch_data(api_url):
    try:
        response = requests.get(api_url, timeout=5)
        response.raise_for_status()  # Raises error for bad responses
        return response.json()
    except requests.exceptions.RequestException as e:
        print(f"API Error: {e}")
```

```
    return None
```

```
data = fetch_data("https://api.example.com/data")
```

3□.Resolving Memory and Performance Issues

Common Causes:

- **Agent consumes too much memory**
- **Slow response times due to inefficient algorithms**
- **Large context windows leading to high computation costs**

Debugging Steps:

Profile memory usage using `memory_profiler`.
Optimize vector embeddings by reducing dimensionality.
Use caching mechanisms to store frequent responses.

Example: Profiling Memory Usage

```python
from memory_profiler import profile


@profile

def run_agent():

    response = my_ai_agent("Analyze this document...")

    return response


run_agent()
```

4▯.Debugging Multi-Agent Coordination Problems

Common Causes:

- **Conflicts in agent roles** (e.g., two agents trying to do the same task).
- **Deadlocks where agents wait for each other indefinitely**.
- **Incorrect message passing between agents**.

Debugging Steps:

Visualize message flow using logs or tracing tools.
Set timeouts for agent responses to avoid deadlocks.
Introduce a hierarchy or priority system to resolve conflicts.

Example: Logging Multi-Agent Interactions

python

```python
def agent_communicate(agent1, agent2, message):

    logging.info(f"{agent1} sent message to {agent2}: {message}")

    response = agent2.receive_message(message)

    logging.info(f"{agent2} responded: {response}")

    return response
```

5▯. Debugging Agent Learning and Adaptation Issues

Common Causes:

- **Reinforcement learning agents not improving over time**.
- **Models overfitting to certain patterns**.
- **Unexpected bias in decision-making**.

Debugging Steps:

Track reward signals in reinforcement learning.
Use explainability tools like SHAP to interpret model predictions.
Regularly retrain with diverse datasets.

Example: Logging Reinforcement Learning Rewards

```python
```

```python
reward_log = []


def reward_function(agent_output, expected_output):
    reward = 1 if agent_output == expected_output else -1
    reward_log.append(reward)
    logging.info(f"Reward: {reward}")
    return reward
```

6□. Handling Security Issues (Injection Attacks, Prompt Manipulation)

Common Causes:

- **Users injecting malicious inputs** to manipulate the agent.
- **SQL injection or code execution via unsafe prompts**.
- **Leakage of sensitive information** due to improper filtering.

Debugging Steps:

Sanitize user inputs before passing them to the model.
Use regex to detect harmful patterns in inputs.
Prevent unintended function execution in agent responses.

Example: Detecting Prompt Injection

```python
```

```
import re


def sanitize_input(user_input):

    if re.search(r"(\bshutdown\b|\bdrop table\b)",
user_input, re.IGNORECASE):

        return "Blocked: Potential malicious input"

    return user_input


print(sanitize_input("Tell me a joke"))

print(sanitize_input("Drop table users"))
```

7□. Debugging Real-World Deployment Issues

Common Causes:

- **Agent behaves differently in production than in testing**.
- **Scaling issues when handling multiple users**.
- **Unreliable cloud-based inference performance**.

Debugging Steps:

Monitor logs in production using tools like **Prometheus** or **ELK Stack**.
Implement feature flags to test new updates gradually.
Run A/B tests to compare different agent versions.

Example: Logging Production Issues

```python

import logging
```

```
logging.basicConfig(filename='agent_logs.log',
level=logging.ERROR)


try:

    response = my_ai_agent("Book me a flight")

    print(response)

except Exception as e:

    logging.error(f"Agent failed: {e}")
```

Debugging AI agents requires **a systematic approach** covering input validation, API testing, performance profiling, agent coordination, security checks, and deployment monitoring. Using these techniques, you can **identify and fix common issues quickly**, ensuring your AI agent remains **robust and reliable**.

9.3 Ensuring Reliability and Robustness in AI Agents

Ensuring the reliability and robustness of AI agents is crucial for their successful deployment in real-world applications. This section explores best practices, testing strategies, and methodologies to enhance the stability and dependability of AI-powered agents.

1□. Implementing Rigorous Testing Protocols

Why?

AI agents need **consistent behavior under different conditions**. Robust testing ensures they handle diverse inputs effectively and produce **reliable results**.

Best Practices

Unit Testing: Validate individual components like NLP pipelines, response generators, and API integrations.
Integration Testing: Ensure agents work correctly with external services (APIs, databases, message queues).
End-to-End Testing: Simulate real-world interactions to verify the agent's complete workflow.
Adversarial Testing: Test with **unexpected or malicious inputs** to ensure security.

Example: Unit Testing an AI Response Function

python

```python
import unittest

def ai_response(user_input):

    return "Hello, how can I assist you?" if "hello" in user_input.lower() else "I don't understand."


class TestAIResponse(unittest.TestCase):

    def test_greeting(self):

        self.assertEqual(ai_response("Hello"), "Hello, how can I assist you?")


    def test_unknown_input(self):

        self.assertEqual(ai_response("Random text"), "I don't understand.")


if __name__ == "__main__":

    unittest.main()
```

2□. Handling Uncertainty and Failures Gracefully

Why?

AI agents **cannot always be 100% accurate**. Implementing fallback mechanisms prevents them from failing silently.

Best Practices

Set confidence thresholds: If an agent's confidence in an answer is low, provide alternative suggestions.
Graceful degradation: Ensure the agent **fails safely** without crashing the system.
Error messaging: Instead of giving incorrect results, provide a **clear error response**.

Example: Handling Low Confidence Scores

python

```
def respond_with_fallback(input_text):

    response, confidence = ai_agent.get_response(input_text)

    if confidence < 0.5:

        return "I'm unsure about that. Would you like me to
rephrase?"

    return response
```

3□. Improving Robustness Against Bias and Data Drift

Why?

Bias in AI agents can lead to **unfair, unethical, or inaccurate** decision-making. Data drift can **degrade performance** over time.

Best Practices

Monitor for bias in training data: Regularly audit datasets to ensure **diversity and fairness**.
Use explainability tools (e.g., SHAP, LIME) to detect patterns in model predictions.
Retrain models periodically to adapt to changing data trends.

Example: Monitoring Model Drift

```python
python


from sklearn.metrics import accuracy_score


def check_model_drift(old_model, new_model, test_data,
test_labels):

    old_acc = accuracy_score(test_labels,
old_model.predict(test_data))

    new_acc = accuracy_score(test_labels,
new_model.predict(test_data))

    drift = old_acc - new_acc

    print(f"Model drift detected: {drift}" if drift > 0.05
else "No significant drift.")
```

4□. Securing AI Agents Against Attacks

Why?

AI agents are vulnerable to **adversarial attacks, prompt injections, and security breaches**.

Best Practices

Sanitize inputs: Prevent prompt injection and command execution attacks.
Limit API access: Use **authentication and authorization** to restrict access

to sensitive data.
Monitor agent activity: Detect anomalies or unusual requests.

Example: Blocking Malicious Inputs

python

```
import re

def sanitize_input(user_input):
    if re.search(r"(shutdown|delete all data|drop table)",
user_input, re.IGNORECASE):
        return "Blocked: Potential malicious input"
    return user_input

print(sanitize_input("Drop table users"))  # Output: Blocked:
Potential malicious input
```

5□. Ensuring Scalability and Performance Efficiency

Why?

As the number of users grows, **agents must maintain speed and reliability**.

Best Practices

Use caching: Store frequent queries to reduce redundant computations.
Optimize vector embeddings: Reduce high-dimensional representations where possible.
Load balance requests: Use **distributed architectures (e.g., Kubernetes, Redis queues)** for scalability.

Example: Implementing Response Caching

```python
python

import functools

cache = {}

def cached_response(func):
    @functools.wraps(func)
    def wrapper(input_text):
        if input_text in cache:
            return cache[input_text]
        response = func(input_text)
        cache[input_text] = response
        return response
    return wrapper

@cached_response
def ai_agent_response(input_text):
    return f"AI-generated response for: {input_text}"

print(ai_agent_response("Hello"))  # First time: Computes response
```

```
print(ai_agent_response("Hello"))  # Second time: Returns
cached response
```

6□. Continuous Monitoring and Logging

Why?

Monitoring logs help **identify issues early** and improve performance over time.

Best Practices

Log input/output interactions: Store logs to analyze agent behavior.
Set up alerting systems: Notify engineers of failures or anomalies.
Use observability tools: Utilize **Grafana, Prometheus, or OpenTelemetry** to monitor performance.

Example: Logging Agent Interactions

python

```
import logging


logging.basicConfig(filename='agent_activity.log',
level=logging.INFO)


def log_interaction(user_input, agent_response):
    logging.info(f"User: {user_input} | Agent:
{agent_response}")


log_interaction("What is AI?", "AI stands for Artificial
Intelligence.")
```

7□. A/B Testing for Continuous Improvement

Why?

Comparing different versions of an AI agent ensures **optimal user experience**.

Best Practices

Deploy multiple versions: Test different model configurations side by side.
Collect user feedback: Use surveys or implicit signals (e.g., response upvotes/downvotes).
Analyze results: Use **metrics like response accuracy and engagement time** to refine the model.

Example: A/B Testing Two AI Agents

python

```python
import random


def get_best_response(user_input):

    agent_version = random.choice(["A", "B"])

    response = ai_agent_vA(user_input) if agent_version ==
"A" else ai_agent_vB(user_input)

    return response, agent_version


print(get_best_response("What is machine learning?"))
```

To ensure **reliability and robustness**, AI agents must: **Undergo extensive testing** (unit, integration, adversarial, A/B testing).
Handle uncertainty with fallback mechanisms and confidence thresholds.
Prevent security vulnerabilities like prompt injection and unauthorized access.
Monitor performance continuously with logging and alerting.
Adapt over time by retraining on new data and preventing model drift.

Following these best practices ensures that AI agents remain **trustworthy, scalable, and secure**, even in dynamic and unpredictable environments.

9.4 Exercise: Test and Debug Your Agent, Document Findings

Objective

In this exercise, you will **test and debug your AI agent**, ensuring it functions correctly under different scenarios. You'll document the process, highlighting any issues found and the solutions implemented.

Step 1: Define the Agent's Functionality

Before testing, clarify what your agent is supposed to do. Assume we have a **customer support AI agent** that:

- Answers common FAQs.
- Redirects users to human support when necessary.
- Fetches real-time weather data using an external API.

Example AI Agent Functionality

python

```
import random


def ai_agent_response(user_input):
```

```python
"""AI agent providing responses based on user input"""
faq_responses = {
    "hello": "Hello! How can I assist you today?",
    "pricing": "Our services start at $10 per month. Do you need a detailed quote?",
    "support": "I will connect you with a human representative."
}


if user_input.lower() in faq_responses:
    return faq_responses[user_input.lower()]


return "I'm sorry, I don't understand. Can you rephrase?"
```

Step 2: Create a Testing Plan

We will perform **three types of testing**:

1□. **Functional Testing**: Does the agent return expected responses?
2□. **Error Handling Tests**: How does it handle unexpected inputs?
3□. **Integration Testing**: Does it work correctly with external services?

Step 3: Write Unit Tests

Use unittest to validate the AI agent's core responses.

python

```python
import unittest


class TestAIAgent(unittest.TestCase):

    def test_greeting(self):

        self.assertEqual(ai_agent_response("hello"), "Hello!
How can I assist you today?")


    def test_pricing(self):

        self.assertEqual(ai_agent_response("pricing"), "Our
services start at $10 per month. Do you need a detailed
quote?")


    def test_unknown_input(self):

        self.assertEqual(ai_agent_response("random query"),
"I'm sorry, I don't understand. Can you rephrase?")


    def test_human_support(self):

        self.assertEqual(ai_agent_response("support"), "I
will connect you with a human representative.")


if __name__ == "__main__":

    unittest.main()
```

Expected Outcome: All tests should pass.

Step 4: Debugging Common Issues

. Potential Issues and Fixes:

Issue	Cause	Solution
AI returns `"None"`	No match in FAQ dictionary	Add a default fallback response
Case sensitivity issues	"Hello" != "hello"	Convert input to lowercase
Misspellings break responses	AI doesn't recognize typos	Implement fuzzy matching (`Levenshtein distance`)
API call failures	Network issues	Use **try-except** to handle API failures

Example Fix for Case Sensitivity

```python
def ai_agent_response(user_input):

    user_input = user_input.lower()   # Convert to lowercase

    return faq_responses.get(user_input, "I'm sorry, I don't understand. Can you rephrase?")
```

Step 5: Perform Integration Testing

If the agent interacts with external APIs (e.g., fetching weather data), test how it handles API failures.

Example: Handling API Errors

```python
import requests
```

```python
def get_weather(city):
    """Fetch weather data from an external API."""
    try:
        response =
requests.get(f"https://api.weatherapi.com/v1/current.json?key
=YOUR_KEY&q={city}")
        response.raise_for_status()
        return response.json()["current"]["temperature"]
    except requests.exceptions.RequestException:
        return "Unable to fetch weather data."


print(get_weather("New York"))  # Test normal case
print(get_weather(""))  # Test empty input
```

Expected Outcome: The agent should return weather data or a proper error message instead of crashing.

Step 6: Stress Testing

- Send **1000+ queries** in rapid succession to check performance.
- Use **randomized inputs** to test robustness.
- Measure **response time**.

```python
python
```

```python
import time
```

```
start_time = time.time()

for _ in range(1000):

    ai_agent_response("hello")  # Repeated queries

end_time = time.time()


print(f"Processed 1000 queries in {end_time - start_time}
seconds.")
```

Step 7: Document Your Findings

Test Type	Scenario	Expected Outcome	Actual Outcome	Status
Functional	User says "hello"	"Hello! How can I assist you today?"	Passed	Passed
Error Handling	AI receives gibberish input	"I don't understand. Can you rephrase?"	Passed	Passed
API Test	Weather API fails	"Unable to fetch weather data."	Passed	Passed
Stress Test	1000 queries	No crashes	Passed	Passed

You've successfully tested and debugged your AI agent!
Ensure documentation is maintained for future debugging.
Next Step: Deploy the agent in a production environment!

Chapter 10: Deploying AI Agents

10.1 Hosting AI Agents on Cloud Platforms

Introduction

Once your AI agent is built, tested, and optimized, the next step is **deployment**. Hosting your agent on a cloud platform ensures **scalability, reliability, and accessibility**. This section explores how to deploy an AI agent on **AWS, Google Cloud, and Azure**.

Step 1: Choosing a Cloud Platform

Each cloud provider offers a variety of services for deploying AI agents. Here's a comparison:

Cloud Provider	Best For	Key AI Services
AWS	Scalable AI applications	AWS Lambda, EC2, SageMaker, Fargate
Google Cloud	AI/ML-powered apps	Vertex AI, Cloud Run, App Engine
Azure	Enterprise solutions	Azure Machine Learning, Azure Functions

Recommendation:

- Use **AWS** for **serverless deployments** (Lambda, Fargate).
- Use **Google Cloud** for **AI-focused workloads** (Vertex AI).
- Use **Azure** for **enterprise-scale AI services**.

Step 2: Containerizing Your AI Agent

Before deployment, package your AI agent in a **Docker container** for easy scalability.

Dockerfile Example

dockerfile

```
# Use a Python base image
FROM python:3.9


# Set working directory
WORKDIR /app


# Copy project files
COPY . .


# Install dependencies
RUN pip install -r requirements.txt


# Expose a port (if running a web server)
EXPOSE 5000


# Start the AI agent
CMD ["python", "agent.py"]
```

Build & Run the Container

bash

```
docker build -t ai-agent .

docker run -p 5000:5000 ai-agent
```

Step 3: Deploying on AWS

Option 1: AWS Lambda (Serverless Deployment)

For lightweight agents, deploy using **AWS Lambda**.

1.**Zip the Project**:

bash

```
zip -r deployment_package.zip
```

2□. **Upload to AWS Lambda** via the console or AWS CLI:

bash

```
aws lambda create-function ¥
    --function-name ai-agent ¥
    --runtime python3.9 ¥
    --role arn:aws:iam::123456789012:role/execution_role ¥
    --handler agent.lambda_handler ¥
    --zip-file fileb://deployment_package.zip
```

3□.**Trigger Lambda** using an API Gateway or EventBridge.

Option 2: AWS EC2 (For Persistent AI Agents)

1☐. Launch an EC2 Instance:

bash

```
aws ec2 run-instances --image-id ami-
xxxxxxxxxxxxxxxxx --count 1 --instance-type
t2.micro --key-name my-key-pair
```

2☐. SSH into the instance:

bash

```
ssh -i my-key-pair.pem ec2-user@your-ec2-public-ip
```

3☐. Deploy your AI agent:

bash

```
git clone https://github.com/your-repo/ai-agent.git
cd ai-agent
pip install -r requirements.txt
python agent.py
```

4☐. Run in Background:

bash

```
nohup python agent.py &
```

Step 4: Deploying on Google Cloud

Option 1: Google Cloud Run (Serverless)

For **stateless AI agents**, use **Cloud Run**:

1️. **Build & Push Docker Image**:

bash

```
gcloud builds submit --tag gcr.io/my-project/ai-agent
```

2️. **Deploy to Cloud Run**:

bash

```
gcloud run deploy ai-agent --image gcr.io/my-project/ai-agent
--platform managed --allow-unauthenticated
```

Option 2: Google Compute Engine (For Persistent Agents)

1️. **Launch a Virtual Machine (VM)**

bash

```
gcloud compute instances create ai-agent-vm --machine-
type=e2-micro
```

2️. **SSH into VM & Deploy Agent**

bash

```
gcloud compute ssh ai-agent-vm
git clone https://github.com/your-repo/ai-agent.git
cd ai-agent
pip install -r requirements.txt
python agent.py
```

Step 5: Deploying on Azure

Option 1: Azure Functions (Serverless)

1☐.**Install Azure CLI**:

bash

```
az login
```

2☐. **Create Function App**:

bash

```
az functionapp create --resource-group MyResourceGroup --
consumption-plan-location eastus --runtime python --name ai-
agent-func
```

3☐. **Deploy Code**:

bash

```
az functionapp deployment source config-zip --resource-group
MyResourceGroup --name ai-agent-func --src
deployment_package.zip
```

Option 2: Azure Virtual Machines

1☐. **Create VM**:

```bash
bash
```

```bash
az vm create --resource-group MyResourceGroup --name ai-
agent-vm --image UbuntuLTS --admin-username azureuser --
generate-ssh-keys
```

2□. SSH into VM & Deploy:

```bash
bash
```

```bash
az vm ssh --name ai-agent-vm

git clone https://github.com/your-repo/ai-agent.git

cd ai-agent

pip install -r requirements.txt

python agent.py
```

Final Thoughts

You have successfully deployed your AI agent!
Next Steps:

- **Monitor Performance** using AWS CloudWatch, Google Logging, or Azure Monitor.
- **Secure the Agent** (next section).
- **Scale the Deployment** using Kubernetes (K8s).

10.2 Setting Up Continuous Integration and Deployment (CI/CD) for AI Agents

Introduction

Once your AI agent is deployed, you need a **Continuous Integration and Deployment (CI/CD)** pipeline to ensure **smooth updates, automation, and**

reliability. This section guides you through setting up a CI/CD pipeline using **GitHub Actions, GitLab CI/CD, and Jenkins**.

Step 1: Choosing a CI/CD Tool

There are several popular CI/CD tools you can use:

Tool	Best For	Integration
GitHub Actions	Easy automation	Works with GitHub
GitLab CI/CD	Self-hosted and cloud options	Built into GitLab
Jenkins	Highly customizable	Works with all repositories
CircleCI	Fast builds	Integrates with AWS, GCP, Azure

Step 2: Setting Up CI/CD with GitHub Actions

GitHub Actions automates **testing, building, and deploying** your AI agent.

1☐.Create a GitHub Workflow

Inside your GitHub repository, create a CI/CD workflow:

File: `.github/workflows/deploy.yml`

```
name: Deploy AI Agent

on:
  push:
    branches:
      - main  # Runs workflow on push to main branch

jobs:
  build:
    runs-on: ubuntu-latest
```

```
steps:
  - name: Checkout Repository
    uses: actions/checkout@v3

  - name: Set up Python
    uses: actions/setup-python@v3
    with:
      python-version: '3.9'

  - name: Install Dependencies
    run: pip install -r requirements.txt

  - name: Run Tests
    run: pytest tests/  # Run automated tests

  - name: Build Docker Image
    run: |
      docker build -t my-ai-agent .
      docker tag my-ai-agent gcr.io/my-project/ai-agent:latest  # Change for AWS/GCP/Azure

  - name: Push to Google Cloud Registry
    run: |
      echo "${{ secrets.GCP_SA_KEY }}" | base64 --decode > gcp-key.json
      gcloud auth activate-service-account --key-file=gcp-key.json
      gcloud builds submit --tag gcr.io/my-project/ai-agent
```

What This Does: Runs on every push to `main`
Installs dependencies
Runs tests using `pytest`
Builds a **Docker container**
Pushes the container to **Google Cloud Registry**

Step 3: Automating Deployment

Now, automate deployment to **AWS, Google Cloud, or Azure**.

253

1️⃣. Deploy to AWS (ECS)

Modify the workflow to deploy the AI agent:

```
- name: Configure AWS CLI
  run: aws configure set aws_access_key_id
${{ secrets.AWS_ACCESS_KEY_ID }} && aws configure
set aws_secret_access_key ${{
secrets.AWS_SECRET_ACCESS_KEY }}

- name: Deploy to AWS ECS
  run: aws ecs update-service --cluster my-
cluster --service ai-agent --force-new-deployment
```

♠ This forces ECS to deploy the latest version of your AI agent.

2️⃣. Deploy to Google Cloud Run

Modify the workflow:

```
- name: Deploy to Cloud Run
  run: gcloud run deploy ai-agent --image
gcr.io/my-project/ai-agent:latest --platform
managed --allow-unauthenticated
```

This redeploys the AI agent on **Google Cloud Run**.

3️⃣. Deploy to Azure App Service

Modify the workflow:

```
- name: Azure Login
  uses: azure/login@v1
  with:
    creds: ${{ secrets.AZURE_CREDENTIALS }}

- name: Deploy to Azure
```

```
    run: |
        az webapp deployment container config --
name my-ai-agent --resource-group my-group --
enable-cd true
```

◆ This enables **auto-deployment** for an Azure **Web App**.

Step 4: Running CI/CD with GitLab CI/CD

For GitLab users, create `.gitlab-ci.yml`:

```
stages:
  - build
  - test
  - deploy

build:
  stage: build
  script:
    - docker build -t my-ai-agent .

test:
  stage: test
  script:
    - pytest tests/

deploy:
  stage: deploy
  only:
    - main
  script:
    - gcloud run deploy ai-agent --image gcr.io/my-
project/ai-agent:latest --platform managed --allow-
unauthenticated
```

Step 5: Using Jenkins for CI/CD

1☐. Install Jenkins Plugins

255

- Docker Pipeline Plugin
- AWS/GCP/Azure Credentials Plugin

2□. Create a Jenkinsfile

```
pipeline {
    agent any

    stages {
        stage('Build') {
            steps {
                sh 'docker build -t my-ai-agent .'
            }
        }

        stage('Test') {
            steps {
                sh 'pytest tests/'
            }
        }

        stage('Deploy') {
            steps {
                sh 'gcloud run deploy ai-agent --
image gcr.io/my-project/ai-agent:latest --platform
managed --allow-unauthenticated'
            }
        }
    }
}
```

Your CI/CD pipeline is now automated!
Every time you push changes, your AI agent is automatically **tested, built, and deployed**.

Next Steps:

- **Monitor Deployments** using AWS CloudWatch, Google Cloud Logging, or Azure Monitor.
- **Enhance Security** (next section).
- **Scale the Pipeline** with Kubernetes (K8s).

10.3 Scaling and Performance Considerations for AI Agents

Scaling AI agents efficiently ensures they can handle increased workloads, maintain low latency, and function reliably across different environments. This section covers **horizontal vs. vertical scaling, optimizing inference performance, caching, load balancing, and distributed deployment strategies**.

---

1. Understanding Scaling Strategies

Scaling AI agents requires two key approaches:

Scaling Type	Description	Best For
Vertical Scaling (Scaling Up)	Increasing system resources (CPU, RAM, GPU)	Small deployments, rapid prototyping
Horizontal Scaling (Scaling Out)	Adding more instances to distribute load	Production-level AI agents, large-scale applications

- **Vertical Scaling**: Add more **RAM, CPU, or GPU** to a single server.
- **Horizontal Scaling**: Deploy multiple **instances** behind a **load balancer**.

Example:
. **GPT-powered chatbots** scale **horizontally** to handle more users, while **edge AI** devices scale **vertically** for better efficiency.

---

2. Optimizing Inference Performance

Inference latency is **critical** for AI agents, especially in real-time applications. Below are some strategies to **reduce response time**:

1 ⬜Model Quantization

- Reduces model size by converting weights to lower precision (e.g., **FP16, INT8**).
- Faster inference on **CPUs and edge devices**.

Example using PyTorch:

```python
```

```python
import torch

from transformers import AutoModel


model = AutoModel.from_pretrained("bert-base-uncased")

quantized_model = torch.quantization.quantize_dynamic(model,
{torch.nn.Linear}, dtype=torch.qint8)
```

◈ **Benefits:** Lower memory usage, faster inference.

2□. Using Optimized Libraries

- **ONNX Runtime**: Runs AI models faster across different platforms.
- **TensorRT (for NVIDIA GPUs)**: Optimizes models for **GPU inference**.

Example using ONNX Runtime:

```python
```

```python
import onnxruntime as ort
```

```
session = ort.InferenceSession("model.onnx",
providers=["CUDAExecutionProvider"])

outputs = session.run(None, {"input": input_data})
```

Speeds up model execution on both CPU and GPU!

3□. Batch Processing

Instead of processing requests **one by one**, group them into **batches**.

Batching reduces latency by processing multiple inputs in a single model call.

Example using FastAPI:

python

```
from fastapi import FastAPI

import torch


app = FastAPI()


@app.post("/predict")
async def predict(inputs: list):
    batch_inputs = torch.tensor(inputs)
    batch_outputs = model(batch_inputs)
    return batch_outputs.tolist()
```

✦ **Best used in APIs that handle multiple users at a time!**

3. Caching and Load Balancing

1□. Implement Caching

Reduce redundant computations by storing **frequent responses**.

- **Redis**: Fast in-memory storage for AI responses.
- **Local File Cache**: Store embeddings/models on disk.

Example using Redis for AI caching:

python

```python
import redis

import json


cache = redis.Redis(host='localhost', port=6379, db=0)


def get_response(query):

    cached = cache.get(query)

    if cached:

        return json.loads(cached)


    response = model.predict(query)

    cache.set(query, json.dumps(response), ex=3600)   # Cache
for 1 hour

    return response
```

◆ Ideal for chatbot AI and recommendation systems!

2□. Load Balancing with Multiple AI Agent Instances

Load balancers distribute incoming traffic **across multiple instances**, preventing overload.

Popular Load Balancers:

- **AWS Elastic Load Balancer (ELB)** – Auto-scales AI agents.
- **NGINX** – Routes traffic between AI instances.
- **Kubernetes Load Balancer** – Distributes requests across AI pods.

Example using NGINX:

```nginx
upstream ai_agents {

    server ai-server-1:5000;

    server ai-server-2:5000;

    server ai-server-3:5000;

}


server {

    listen 80;

    location / {

        proxy_pass http://ai_agents;

    }

}
```

♦ **Distributes traffic efficiently across multiple AI backends!**

---

4. Distributed Deployment Strategies

For large-scale AI systems, **deploy across multiple regions or clouds**.

1□. Multi-Cloud AI Deployment

- Deploy AI agents on **AWS, GCP, and Azure** for redundancy.
- **Example**: AWS Lambda for real-time responses, GCP for batch
  inference.

2□. Kubernetes (K8s) for AI Agents

- Runs AI models in **containers** for better scalability.
- Uses **Horizontal Pod Autoscaler (HPA)** to increase replicas when
  needed.

Example: Kubernetes scaling AI agents

```yaml
apiVersion: autoscaling/v2beta2

kind: HorizontalPodAutoscaler

metadata:

  name: ai-agent-hpa

spec:

  scaleTargetRef:

    apiVersion: apps/v1

    kind: Deployment

    name: ai-agent
```

```
minReplicas: 2

maxReplicas: 10

metrics:

  - type: Resource

    resource:

      name: cpu

      target:

        type: Utilization

        averageUtilization: 70
```

◆ **Auto-scales AI agent replicas when CPU usage exceeds 70%!**

---

5. Monitoring AI Agent Performance

Use monitoring tools to track **latency, errors, and response times**.

Recommended Monitoring Tools:

- **Prometheus + Grafana** – Tracks real-time AI performance.
- **New Relic / Datadog** – AI monitoring on cloud platforms.
- **AWS CloudWatch / Google Cloud Logging** – Logs inference times.

Example: Monitor AI response time with Prometheus

```yaml
- job_name: 'ai-agent'

  static_configs:

    - targets: ['localhost:8000']
```

◆ Ensures AI agents maintain consistent performance!

Scaling AI agents efficiently ensures they remain responsive and cost-effective!

Key Takeaways: Scale horizontally for high workloads.
Optimize inference using quantization, TensorRT, and ONNX.
Use caching (Redis) and **load balancers** (NGINX, Kubernetes).
Monitor agent performance with **Prometheus, Grafana, or Datadog.**

10.4 Exercise: Deploy Your AI Agent and Monitor Performance

In this hands-on exercise, you'll deploy an AI agent to a cloud platform, set up monitoring, and optimize its performance. You'll achieve this by:

1. Deploying the agent using **FastAPI and Docker**.
2. Hosting it on **AWS/GCP/Azure** (or locally with **NGINX**).
3. Implementing **monitoring with Prometheus and Grafana**.
4. Optimizing performance using **caching and scaling techniques**.

Step 1: Create a Simple AI Agent API

We'll create a **FastAPI** server that serves an AI agent.

Install Dependencies

```bash
pip install fastapi uvicorn transformers torch
```

AI Agent Code (FastAPI)

```python
```

```python
from fastapi import FastAPI
from transformers import pipeline


app = FastAPI()
ai_agent = pipeline("text-generation", model="gpt2")


@app.get("/generate/")
def generate(prompt: str):
    response = ai_agent(prompt, max_length=50,
num_return_sequences=1)
    return {"generated_text": response[0]["generated_text"]}
```

Test locally by running:

```bash
bash
```

```bash
uvicorn main:app --host 0.0.0.0 --port 8000
```

Visit: http://localhost:8000/docs

Step 2: Containerize Your AI Agent

Create a Dockerfile

```dockerfile
dockerfile
```

```
FROM python:3.9
```

```
WORKDIR /app
```

```
COPY requirements.txt .
```

```
RUN pip install -r requirements.txt
```

```
COPY . .
```

```
CMD ["uvicorn", "main:app", "--host", "0.0.0.0", "--port",
"8000"]
```

Build and Run Docker

```
bash
```

```
docker build -t ai-agent .
```

```
docker run -p 8000:8000 ai-agent
```

Your AI agent is now running inside a Docker container!

Step 3: Deploy to Cloud

You can deploy your AI agent to **AWS (ECS), GCP (Cloud Run), or Azure (Container Apps)**.

Deploy to AWS

```
bash
```

```
aws ecr create-repository --repository-name ai-agent
```

```bash
docker tag ai-agent:latest <aws-account-
id>.dkr.ecr.<region>.amazonaws.com/ai-agent
```

```bash
docker push <aws-account-
id>.dkr.ecr.<region>.amazonaws.com/ai-agent
```

Deploy the image to **AWS ECS or Lambda**.

Deploy to GCP Cloud Run

bash

```bash
gcloud builds submit --tag gcr.io/<project-id>/ai-agent
```

```bash
gcloud run deploy ai-agent --image gcr.io/<project-id>/ai-
agent --platform managed
```

Now, your AI agent is live on the cloud!

Step 4: Set Up Monitoring

1 Install Prometheus for Monitoring

bash

```bash
docker run -d -p 9090:9090 --name prometheus -v
prometheus.yml:/etc/prometheus/prometheus.yml prom/prometheus
```

2 Install Grafana for Visualizing Metrics

bash

```bash
docker run -d -p 3000:3000 --name=grafana grafana/grafana
```

Monitor API requests, latency, and performance!

Step 5: Optimize Performance

   1. **Enable Caching (Redis)**

bash

```
docker run -d -p 6379:6379 redis
```

python

```python
import redis

cache = redis.Redis(host="localhost", port=6379, db=0)

def get_response(prompt):
    cached = cache.get(prompt)
    if cached:
        return cached.decode("utf-8")

    response = ai_agent(prompt, max_length=50,
num_return_sequences=1)[0]["generated_text"]
    cache.set(prompt, response, ex=3600)   # Cache for 1 hour
    return response
```

   2. **Use Load Balancing (NGINX)**

nginx

```
upstream ai_agents {

    server ai-agent-1:8000;

    server ai-agent-2:8000;

}


server {

    listen 80;

    location / {

        proxy_pass http://ai_agents;

    }

}
```

This allows multiple instances to handle more requests efficiently!

Complete the following:

1. Deploy the AI agent on a cloud platform.
2. Set up monitoring (Prometheus, Grafana).
3. Optimize performance (Redis caching, NGINX load balancing).
4. **Document your findings:**
    - What were the response times before and after optimization?
    - Did caching reduce inference time?
    - How does load balancing affect performance?

Chapter 11: Ethical Considerations in AI Agent Development

11.1 Addressing Bias in AI Agents

AI agents can inadvertently learn and reinforce biases from training data, leading to unfair or unethical outcomes. Addressing bias is crucial to ensure fairness, transparency, and reliability in AI-driven decision-making.

Understanding Bias in AI Agents

Bias in AI arises from multiple sources, including:

1. **Data Bias** – Training data may reflect historical or societal prejudices.
2. **Algorithmic Bias** – Certain model architectures may favor specific patterns.
3. **User Interaction Bias** – AI adapts to user behaviors, which may reinforce bias over time.
4. **Deployment Bias** – The real-world application of AI may not match the training environment, leading to skewed outcomes.

Example: Biased Resume Screening

An AI trained on past hiring data may prefer candidates based on gender, ethnicity, or school attended if such biases were present in historical hiring decisions.

Strategies to Mitigate Bias in AI Agents

1□. Data Collection and Preprocessing

- **Diverse Datasets:** Ensure representation across demographics.
- **Data Augmentation:** Balance underrepresented classes through synthetic data.

- **Bias Auditing Tools:** Use AI fairness tools like IBM AI Fairness 360 or Google's What-If Tool.

2️. Algorithmic Fairness Techniques

- **Fair Representation Learning:** Techniques like re-weighting samples to prevent disproportionate representation.
- **Adversarial Debiasing:** Training a second model to detect and minimize bias signals in predictions.

3️. Transparent Model Evaluation

- **Fairness Metrics:** Use statistical metrics like:
  - **Demographic Parity** – Predictions should be independent of sensitive attributes.
  - **Equalized Odds** – False positive/negative rates should be similar across groups.
- **Explainability Techniques:** Use SHAP (SHapley Additive exPlanations) or LIME (Local Interpretable Model-agnostic Explanations) to interpret model behavior.

4️. Continuous Monitoring & User Feedback

- **Bias Detection Pipelines:** Continuously audit AI outputs for disparities.
- **User Feedback Mechanisms:** Allow users to report unfair decisions and retrain models accordingly.

Implementation Example: Checking for Bias in an AI Model

Step 1: Install Required Libraries

bash

```
pip install pandas numpy sklearn aif360
```

Step 2: Load a Sample Biased Dataset

```python
import pandas as pd
from aif360.datasets import StandardDataset

# Sample biased hiring dataset
data = pd.DataFrame({
    "Gender": ["Male", "Female", "Male", "Female", "Male"],
    "Score": [85, 90, 78, 88, 82],
    "Hired": [1, 0, 1, 0, 1]  # Hiring biased against women
})

# Convert to AIF360 StandardDataset format
dataset = StandardDataset(data, label_name="Hired",
protected_attribute_names=["Gender"])

print("Dataset loaded successfully.")
```

Step 3: Apply Bias Detection Metrics

```python
from aif360.metrics import BinaryLabelDatasetMetric

# Calculate bias metrics
```

```
metric = BinaryLabelDatasetMetric(dataset,
privileged_groups=[{"Gender": "Male"}],
unprivileged_groups=[{"Gender": "Female"}])

print(f"Disparate Impact: {metric.disparate_impact()}")
```

11.2 Ensuring Privacy and Security in AI Agents

AI agents handle sensitive data, making privacy and security essential considerations in their development. Ensuring these safeguards prevents unauthorized access, data breaches, and misuse of personal information.

Key Privacy and Security Challenges

1. **Data Leakage** – AI models may inadvertently expose sensitive information.
2. **Unauthorized Access** – Weak authentication can lead to data theft.
3. **Adversarial Attacks** – Malicious inputs can manipulate AI outputs.
4. **Model Inversion Attacks** – Attackers can infer training data from a model.
5. **Compliance Issues** – Regulations like **GDPR**, **CCPA**, and **HIPAA** require strict data handling.

Strategies for Ensuring Privacy and Security

1□. Data Protection Techniques

- **Data Anonymization** – Remove or mask personal identifiers in datasets.
- **Differential Privacy** – Introduce statistical noise to prevent data traceability.
- **Encryption** – Encrypt stored and transmitted data using AES-256 or TLS protocols.
- **Federated Learning** – Train models without sharing raw data across devices.

2□. Secure Model Deployment

- **Access Control** – Implement **role-based access control (RBAC)**.
- **API Security** – Use OAuth 2.0, API keys, or JWT authentication for secure API access.
- **Container Security** – Use Kubernetes RBAC, secrets management, and security policies.
- **Monitoring & Logging** – Implement logging tools like **Splunk** or **AWS CloudTrail**.

3□. Preventing Adversarial Attacks

- **Input Validation** – Sanitize user input to prevent injection attacks.
- **Adversarial Training** – Train models against adversarial perturbations.
- **Rate Limiting** – Restrict API requests to prevent brute-force attacks.
- **AI Explainability** – Use interpretability tools to detect unexpected behaviors.

4□. Compliance with Privacy Regulations

- **GDPR** (General Data Protection Regulation) – Ensure users can request data deletion.
- **CCPA** (California Consumer Privacy Act) – Provide transparency on data usage.
- **HIPAA** (Health Insurance Portability and Accountability Act) – Encrypt and limit healthcare data access.

Implementation Example: Securing an AI API

Step 1: Install Required Libraries

bash

```
pip install fastapi pydantic uvicorn pyjwt cryptography
```

Step 2: Create a Secure API with Authentication

python

```python
from fastapi import FastAPI, Depends, HTTPException
from pydantic import BaseModel
import jwt
from datetime import datetime, timedelta


# Secret key for JWT
SECRET_KEY = "your_secure_secret_key"


app = FastAPI()


class AuthRequest(BaseModel):
    username: str
    password: str


def create_token(data: dict, expires_delta: int = 30):
    expire = datetime.utcnow() +
timedelta(minutes=expires_delta)
    data.update({"exp": expire})
    return jwt.encode(data, SECRET_KEY, algorithm="HS256")


@app.post("/login")
def login(auth: AuthRequest):
```

```python
    if auth.username == "admin" and auth.password ==
"securepassword":

        token = create_token({"sub": auth.username})

        return {"access_token": token}

    raise HTTPException(status_code=401, detail="Invalid
credentials")


@app.get("/secure-data")

def get_secure_data(token: str = Depends(create_token)):

    try:

        jwt.decode(token, SECRET_KEY, algorithms=["HS256"])

        return {"message": "Access granted to secure data"}

    except jwt.ExpiredSignatureError:

        raise HTTPException(status_code=401, detail="Token
expired")

    except jwt.InvalidTokenError:

        raise HTTPException(status_code=401, detail="Invalid
token")
```

This API uses JWT authentication to protect secure data access.

Key Takeaways

- Use **data anonymization, encryption, and federated learning** to protect user privacy.
- Secure AI deployments with **RBAC, OAuth, and API rate limiting**.

- Prevent adversarial attacks using **input validation, adversarial training, and monitoring**.
- Follow **GDPR, CCPA, and HIPAA** compliance to avoid legal risks.

11.3 Responsible Development and Deployment Guidelines for AI Agents

Developing and deploying AI agents responsibly ensures that they are fair, transparent, and aligned with ethical principles. This section outlines best practices for responsible AI development, covering key areas such as fairness, accountability, security, transparency, and regulatory compliance.

1. Principles of Responsible AI Development

Responsible AI must adhere to ethical guidelines that prioritize human welfare. The core principles include:

- **Fairness**: Avoid biases in training data and model predictions.
- **Accountability**: Define responsibility in AI decision-making.
- **Transparency**: Make AI processes explainable and interpretable.
- **Security**: Protect user data and prevent vulnerabilities.
- **Compliance**: Follow legal and ethical guidelines.

2. Ensuring Fairness and Reducing Bias

AI models can unintentionally discriminate based on race, gender, or other attributes. To mitigate this:

Bias Detection and Mitigation Techniques

1. **Diverse and Representative Training Data**
   - Ensure datasets are balanced across different demographics.
   - Use de-biasing techniques like **re-sampling** or **adversarial training**.
2. **Fairness-Aware Algorithms**
   - Use fairness-aware training methods such as **equalized odds** or **demographic parity**.

o Apply post-processing techniques to adjust model outputs.
3. **Regular Bias Audits**
   o Use fairness testing tools like **IBM AI Fairness 360** or **Google's What-If Tool**.
   o Analyze model predictions across demographic groups.

---

3. Security and Privacy Best Practices

AI agents often interact with sensitive data. Implement the following best practices:

Secure Data Handling

- **Encrypt stored and transmitted data** (e.g., AES-256 encryption).
- **Minimize data collection**—only store necessary user inputs.
- **Anonymize sensitive information** before processing.

Secure API Access

- Use **API keys and OAuth authentication**.
- Store API keys securely in **environment variables** instead of hardcoding them.

Example: Using .env files for API security

python

```
import os

from dotenv import load_dotenv


load_dotenv()  # Load environment variables


API_KEY = os.getenv("API_KEY")  # Securely retrieve API key
```

Prevent AI Model Exploitation

- Implement **rate limiting** and **access control** to prevent API abuse.
- Use **input sanitization** to avoid adversarial attacks.

---

4. Transparency and Explainability

AI models must be interpretable, especially in critical applications like healthcare or finance.

Methods for AI Explainability

- **SHAP (Shapley Additive Explanations)** to explain model predictions.
- **LIME (Local Interpretable Model-agnostic Explanations)** to understand decision-making.

Example: Using SHAP to explain AI model decisions

python

```
import shap

import xgboost

import numpy as np


# Sample dataset

X_train = np.random.rand(100, 5)

y_train = np.random.randint(2, size=100)


# Train a model

model = xgboost.XGBClassifier()
```

```
model.fit(X_train, y_train)


# Explain predictions

explainer = shap.Explainer(model)

shap_values = explainer(X_train)


# Visualize

shap.summary_plot(shap_values, X_train)
```

This helps users understand why an AI agent made a particular decision.

📜 5. Regulatory Compliance

AI agents should comply with local and global AI regulations:

Key AI Regulations

Regulation	Key Focus
GDPR (Europe)	Data privacy, user consent, and right to be forgotten.
CCPA (California, USA)	Data protection and user rights.
AI Act (EU)	Risk-based AI classification and compliance.

Checklist for AI Compliance

- Obtain **explicit user consent** for data collection.
- Allow users to **opt-out of AI-driven decisions**.
- Maintain **audit logs** to track AI decisions.

6. Responsible Deployment Practices

Deployment should consider ethical, legal, and operational risks.

Best Practices

1. **Continuous Monitoring & Testing**
   - Regularly audit AI performance to detect **drift** or **unexpected biases**.
   - Implement **automated retraining pipelines** for model updates.
2. **Human-in-the-Loop (HITL)**
   - Ensure AI agents **require human approval** in high-risk scenarios (e.g., medical AI).
   - Provide override mechanisms where humans can **correct AI errors**.
3. **Version Control & Rollbacks**
   - Maintain different AI model versions for **comparison and rollbacks**.
   - Use **A/B testing** to validate changes before deployment.

Summary: Key Takeaways

Ensure fairness by using **bias audits** and **fairness-aware algorithms**.
Strengthen security through **encryption**, **API protection**, and **access controls**.
Improve transparency with **explainability tools** like **SHAP** and **LIME**.
Follow **GDPR, CCPA, and AI Act** compliance regulations.
Deploy responsibly using **continuous monitoring** and **human oversight**.

11.4 Exercise: Implement Ethical Practices in Your AI Agent and Assess for Bias

Objective

In this exercise, you will integrate ethical AI practices into your AI agent by:

1. Identifying and mitigating bias in the model's responses.
2. Ensuring fairness and transparency in decision-making.
3. Implementing privacy and security measures.
4. Evaluating ethical compliance using automated tools.

Step 1: Identify Potential Bias in Your AI Agent

Before implementing ethical safeguards, analyze how your AI agent might be biased. Bias can arise due to:

- **Training Data Bias** (e.g., dataset skews towards certain demographics)
- **Algorithmic Bias** (e.g., decision rules favoring one outcome)
- **Deployment Bias** (e.g., unintended harmful behaviors in real-world applications)

Task: Run a fairness test on your agent's responses.

Example: Testing for Bias in Sentiment Analysis

python

```
from transformers import pipeline


# Load a sentiment analysis model
classifier = pipeline("sentiment-analysis")


# Sample inputs with potential bias
texts = [

    "A young Black man is walking in the park.",
```

```
"A young White man is walking in the park.",

"A woman is applying for a leadership position.",

"A man is applying for a leadership position."
]


# Run the model

results = [classifier(text)[0] for text in texts]


# Display results

for text, result in zip(texts, results):

    print(f"Text: {text} -> Sentiment: {result['label']}
(Confidence: {result['score']:.2f})")
```

Analyze if similar inputs result in different sentiment scores due to implicit biases.

Step 2: Implement Bias Mitigation Techniques

Once you've identified biases, apply strategies to reduce them.

1□. Diverse and Balanced Training Data

- Use datasets that represent a variety of demographics, languages, and perspectives.
- Apply **oversampling** or **undersampling** techniques to balance dataset distribution.

2□. Fairness Constraints in Models

- Use **Adversarial Debiasing** to ensure fairness.

- Train models with **demographic parity** constraints.

3□. Implement Ethical Guidelines in Responses

- Avoid harmful stereotypes by using **filtering techniques**.
- Apply **reinforcement learning from human feedback (RLHF)** to ensure ethical behavior.

Task: Modify your AI agent to filter biased or harmful responses.

Example: Implementing a Bias Filter

python

```python
def bias_filter(response):

    bias_keywords = ["gender", "race", "ethnicity"]

    if any(word in response.lower() for word in
bias_keywords):

        return "I'm designed to provide unbiased responses.
Can I help with something else?"

    return response



# Test the function

user_input = "Who is better at coding, men or women?"

ai_response = "Men are better at coding than women."

filtered_response = bias_filter(ai_response)



print(filtered_response)  # Expected: "I'm designed to
provide unbiased responses..."
```

This function detects and removes biased responses before they reach the user.

Step 3: Implement Privacy and Security Best Practices

Ethical AI also involves protecting user data.

Secure Data Handling

- **Use Encryption:** Store sensitive data using AES-256.
- **Minimize Data Retention:** Delete logs after a set period.
- **Anonymization:** Remove personally identifiable information (PII).

Task: Secure API keys and sensitive data.

Example: Secure API Key Storage Using Environment Variables

python

```
import os

from dotenv import load_dotenv


load_dotenv()  # Load environment variables from a .env file


API_KEY = os.getenv("API_KEY")  # Securely retrieve API key


# Use API_KEY securely without exposing it in code
```

This method prevents hardcoding sensitive credentials in your codebase.

Step 4: Evaluate Ethical Compliance

To ensure ethical AI, measure fairness and transparency using automated tools.

1️.IBM AI Fairness 360 Toolkit

- Evaluates fairness metrics like disparate impact and equalized odds.

2️Google What-If Tool

- Helps visualize model fairness and bias in predictions.

Task: Use an automated fairness tool to assess your AI model.

Key Takeaways

- **Bias detection** is the first step in ensuring fairness.
- **Bias mitigation techniques** include diverse datasets, filtering, and adversarial debiasing.
- **Secure data handling** is crucial for ethical AI.
- **Fairness evaluation tools** help ensure ethical compliance.

Chapter 12: Real-World Use Cases of AI Agents

AI agents are transforming industries by automating tasks, enhancing efficiency, and improving decision-making. This chapter presents real-world case studies across multiple domains, including customer support, data analysis, healthcare, finance, and automation.

12.1 AI Agents in Customer Support

Use Case: AI Chatbots for Automated Customer Service

Example: Chatbot for E-commerce Support

Company: Amazon
Solution: Amazon uses AI-powered chatbots to handle customer inquiries, returns, and recommendations.
Technology Used: NLP models like GPT, sentiment analysis, and intent recognition.

Impact:

- Reduced response time from **minutes to seconds**.
- Automated resolution for **60% of customer queries**.
- Improved **customer satisfaction scores by 20%**.

. Key Takeaways:

- AI chatbots reduce human workload and improve service availability.
- Integrating **sentiment analysis** can improve customer experience.

Implementation Example: Building a Customer Support Chatbot

python

```
from langchain.chat_models import ChatOpenAI

from langchain.schema import AIMessage, HumanMessage
```

```python
# Initialize AI chatbot

chatbot = ChatOpenAI(model="gpt-4")


# Simulate a customer query

response = chatbot([HumanMessage(content="Where is my order?")])

print(response.content)
```

This chatbot can be deployed on platforms like WhatsApp, Messenger, or Slack.

AI Agents in Data Analysis

Use Case: AI for Business Intelligence

Example: AI-Powered Sales Forecasting

Company: Salesforce
Solution: Uses AI-powered analytics to predict sales trends based on historical data.
Technology Used: Machine learning models, time-series forecasting.

Impact:

- Increased **forecast accuracy by 35%**.
- Helped businesses optimize **inventory and resource planning**.

. Key Takeaways:

- AI can process vast amounts of data for accurate forecasting.
- Combining **real-time data streams** enhances predictions.

Implementation Example: AI-Powered Sales Forecasting

```python
python
```

```python
import pandas as pd
from sklearn.linear_model import LinearRegression


# Sample sales data
data = {'Month': [1, 2, 3, 4, 5], 'Sales': [500, 550, 620, 700, 750]}
df = pd.DataFrame(data)


# Train a simple predictive model
X = df[['Month']]
y = df['Sales']
model = LinearRegression()
model.fit(X, y)


# Predict next month's sales
next_month = [[6]]
predicted_sales = model.predict(next_month)
print(f"Predicted sales for next month: {predicted_sales[0]}")
```

AI-powered forecasting can help businesses make data-driven decisions.

AI Agents in Healthcare

Use Case: AI for Medical Diagnosis

Example: AI-Powered Radiology Assistance

Company: Google Health
Solution: Uses deep learning to detect cancer from radiology scans.
Technology Used: CNN-based image recognition models.

Impact:

- Increased **diagnostic accuracy by 94%**.
- Reduced **false positives and false negatives** in scans.

. **Key Takeaways:**

- AI enhances **early detection** and **reduces human errors**.
- Integrating AI with **electronic health records (EHRs)** improves efficiency.

Implementation Example: AI-Powered Image Classification for Medical Diagnosis

python

```
from tensorflow import keras

from tensorflow.keras.models import load_model

import numpy as np


# Load pre-trained medical AI model

model = load_model("radiology_ai_model.h5")


# Simulated input (reshaped image data)

image_data = np.random.rand(1, 224, 224, 3)  # Example
medical image
```

```
# Make a prediction

prediction = model.predict(image_data)

print(f"Diagnosis probability: {prediction[0][0]}")
```

AI can assist doctors in diagnosing diseases faster and more accurately.

AI Agents in Finance

Use Case: AI for Fraud Detection

Example: AI in Credit Card Fraud Prevention

Company: PayPal
Solution: Uses machine learning to analyze transactions and detect fraudulent patterns.
Technology Used: Anomaly detection, behavior analysis.

Impact:

- Reduced fraudulent transactions by **82%**.
- Saved businesses **millions of dollars** annually.

. Key Takeaways:

- AI models can detect fraud patterns in real-time.
- Behavioral analysis helps identify **high-risk transactions**.

Implementation Example: AI-Based Fraud Detection

```python
from sklearn.ensemble import IsolationForest

import numpy as np
```

```
# Simulated transaction data

transactions = np.array([[200], [220], [250], [5000], [230],
[240]])  # One abnormal transaction


# Train anomaly detection model

model = IsolationForest(contamination=0.1)

model.fit(transactions)


# Predict fraud

predictions = model.predict([[5000]])  # High-value
transaction

print("Fraud detected" if predictions[0] == -1 else
"Transaction approved")
```

AI-based fraud detection can prevent financial losses.

AI Agents in Automation

 Use Case: AI-Powered Robotic Process Automation (RPA)

Example: Automating Document Processing in Banking

Company: JPMorgan Chase
Solution: Uses AI to analyze and process legal documents.
Technology Used: NLP and optical character recognition (OCR).

Impact:

- Reduced manual effort by **360,000 hours per year**.

- Improved accuracy and efficiency of document processing.

. Key Takeaways:

- AI speeds up labor-intensive administrative tasks.
- RPA combined with AI enables **end-to-end automation**.

Implementation Example: Automating Document Processing

```python
import pytesseract
from PIL import Image

# Load and process an image of a document
image = Image.open("sample_document.png")
text = pytesseract.image_to_string(image)

print("Extracted text:", text)
```

AI can automate data extraction from documents, emails, and invoices.

Summary: AI in Action

Industry	Use Case	Technology	Impact
Customer Support	AI chatbots	NLP, Sentiment Analysis	Faster response time, 60% automation
Data Analysis	Sales forecasting	ML models, time-series data	35% improved accuracy
Healthcare	AI-assisted diagnosis	Deep learning, CNNs	94% accuracy in scans
Finance	Fraud detection	Anomaly detection	82% fraud reduction
Automation	Document processing	NLP, OCR	Saved 360,000 hours/year

---

Next Step: Implement AI in Your Project

Now that you've seen real-world applications, try integrating AI into your own project!
Choose a domain (Customer Support, Finance, etc.).
Select an AI technique (NLP, ML, Anomaly Detection, etc.).
Build and test your AI agent using practical examples from this chapter.

◆ **Exercise:** Identify a real-world problem and develop an AI agent to solve it!

12.2 Best Practices for Designing AI Agents for Specific Industries

AI agents play a crucial role in various industries, automating workflows, enhancing decision-making, and improving efficiency. However, designing agents tailored for specific industries requires a strategic approach. This section outlines **best practices** for developing AI agents across key industries: **customer support, healthcare, finance, manufacturing, education, and cybersecurity**.

Customer Support: AI-Powered Virtual Assistants

Best Practices

1. **Use NLP and Sentiment Analysis**
   - Train chatbots using domain-specific datasets to understand industry jargon.
   - Implement **sentiment analysis** to adjust responses based on customer emotions.
2. **Seamless Integration with CRMs**
   - Connect AI agents with **Salesforce, HubSpot, or Zendesk** for real-time customer data.
3. **Human Escalation Mechanism**
   - Ensure the AI agent can **seamlessly transfer** complex queries to human agents.
4. **Multi-Channel Support**
   - Deploy AI chatbots on **websites, mobile apps, WhatsApp, and voice assistants**.

Implementation Example: AI Chatbot for Customer Support

```python
from langchain.chat_models import ChatOpenAI
from langchain.schema import HumanMessage

chatbot = ChatOpenAI(model="gpt-4")

response = chatbot([HumanMessage(content="I need help with my order.")])
print(response.content)
```

Deploy on Slack, WhatsApp, or Messenger to automate support.

. Healthcare: AI-Assisted Diagnosis and Patient Support

Best Practices

1. **Regulatory Compliance**
   - Ensure compliance with **HIPAA, GDPR, or other healthcare regulations**.
   - Implement **data encryption and secure storage** of patient records.
2. **Explainable AI (XAI) in Medical Decisions**
   - Use interpretable models to **explain diagnoses and recommendations**.
3. **Integration with EHR Systems**
   - AI agents should connect with **Electronic Health Records (EHRs)** to assist doctors.
4. **Human-AI Collaboration**
   - AI should provide **diagnostic assistance**, but the final decision should remain with doctors.

Implementation Example: AI-Powered Medical Diagnosis

python

```python
from tensorflow.keras.models import load_model
import numpy as np

model = load_model("medical_ai_model.h5")

image_data = np.random.rand(1, 224, 224, 3)  # Simulated
radiology scan
prediction = model.predict(image_data)

print(f"Diagnosis confidence: {prediction[0][0]:.2f}")
```

AI assists in early disease detection but requires human oversight.

Finance: Fraud Detection and Risk Management

Best Practices

1. **Anomaly Detection for Fraud Prevention**
   o Use **unsupervised learning models** (e.g., Isolation Forest) to detect suspicious transactions.
2. **Real-Time Transaction Monitoring**
   o Implement **real-time alerts** for high-risk activities.
3. **Bias Mitigation in Loan Approvals**
   o Ensure models **do not discriminate** based on race, gender, or age.
4. **High-Frequency Trading (HFT) Optimization**
   o AI trading bots should **follow regulatory guidelines** to prevent market manipulation.

Implementation Example: AI for Fraud Detection

python

```python
from sklearn.ensemble import IsolationForest
import numpy as np


transactions = np.array([[200], [220], [250], [5000], [230],
[240]])   # One abnormal transaction


model = IsolationForest(contamination=0.1)
model.fit(transactions)


predictions = model.predict([[5000]])   # High-value
transaction
print("Fraud detected" if predictions[0] == -1 else
"Transaction approved")
```

AI helps financial institutions prevent fraud and manage risk.

. Manufacturing: AI-Powered Process Automation

Best Practices

1. **Predictive Maintenance for Equipment Monitoring**
   o Use AI models to **predict machine failures** before they
     occur.
2. **AI in Quality Control**
   o Implement **computer vision** to detect defects in real-time.
3. **Supply Chain Optimization**

- o AI can analyze demand trends and **optimize inventory management**.
4. **Human-Safety Measures**
   - o Use **AI-powered sensors** to detect worker safety violations.

Implementation Example: Predictive Maintenance for Machines

python

```
import numpy as np

from sklearn.linear_model import LogisticRegression


sensor_data = np.array([[10, 0], [50, 1], [30, 0], [80, 1]])
# [vibration level, failure (1/0)]

X, y = sensor_data[:, 0].reshape(-1, 1), sensor_data[:, 1]


model = LogisticRegression()

model.fit(X, y)


failure_risk = model.predict([[60]])   # Predict risk for
machine at 60% vibration level

print("High failure risk" if failure_risk[0] == 1 else "Low
failure risk")
```

AI improves machine efficiency and reduces downtime.

Education: Personalized Learning Agents

Best Practices

1. **Adaptive Learning Systems**
   o AI should tailor content based on **student progress and learning speed**.
2. **AI-Powered Tutoring Assistants**
   o Implement **virtual tutors** that adapt to individual learning styles.
3. **Plagiarism and Cheating Detection**
   o AI should identify **copy-pasting** or unusual writing patterns.
4. **Natural Language Processing for Student Feedback**
   o AI should analyze student **feedback sentiment** for course improvements.

Implementation Example: AI-Powered Adaptive Learning

python

```python
import random


def suggest_learning_material(score):

    if score < 50:

        return "Suggested: Beginner-level content"

    elif 50 <= score < 80:

        return "Suggested: Intermediate-level content"

    else:

        return "Suggested: Advanced-level content"


student_score = random.randint(0, 100)

print(f"Student Score: {student_score} -
{suggest_learning_material(student_score)}")
```

AI enables personalized learning experiences for students.

🔐 Cybersecurity: AI in Threat Detection

Best Practices

1. **Real-Time Threat Detection**
   - Use **behavior-based AI models** to detect anomalies.
2. **Automated Security Updates**
   - AI should **scan vulnerabilities** and suggest patch updates.
3. **AI-Powered Phishing Detection**
   - AI models should detect **malicious emails and links**.
4. **Identity Verification and Access Control**
   - Use **biometric authentication** for AI-driven security.

Implementation Example: AI for Malware Detection

python

```python
from sklearn.ensemble import RandomForestClassifier

import numpy as np


# Simulated malware dataset

data = np.array([[1, 0, 0], [1, 1, 0], [0, 0, 1], [0, 1, 1]])
# [Suspicious, FileSize, Encrypted]

labels = [1, 1, 0, 0]  # 1 = Malware, 0 = Safe


model = RandomForestClassifier()

model.fit(data, labels)
```

```
# Test on a new file

malware_prediction = model.predict([[1, 1, 1]])  # Highly
suspicious file

print("Malware detected!" if malware_prediction[0] == 1 else
"File is safe.")
```

AI strengthens cybersecurity by detecting threats proactively.

Summary: AI Best Practices by Industry

Industry	Best Practices	Key Benefits
Customer Support	NLP, Sentiment Analysis, CRM Integration	24/7 automated responses
Healthcare	Explainable AI, Regulatory Compliance	Early disease detection
Finance	Fraud detection, Bias mitigation	Reduced financial risks
Manufacturing	Predictive Maintenance, AI Safety	Increased efficiency
Education	Personalized Learning, AI Tutors	Improved student engagement
Cybersecurity	AI Threat Detection, Phishing Prevention	Enhanced security

Exercise 12.3: Design an AI Agent for a Real-World Scenario and Document Your Design Choices

Objective

In this exercise, you will design an AI agent for a real-world scenario, considering its purpose, architecture, data handling, and deployment. Your goal is to **document the key design choices** and justify why they are suitable for the chosen industry.

Step 1: Select a Real-World Scenario

Choose an industry and use case for your AI agent. Here are some examples:

Industry	AI Agent Use Case
Customer Support	Virtual assistant for handling customer queries
Healthcare	AI-powered medical diagnosis chatbot
Finance	Fraud detection agent for real-time transactions
Manufacturing	Predictive maintenance system for factory equipment
Education	Personalized learning assistant for students
Cybersecurity	AI-driven threat detection and anomaly monitoring

Example Selection: "Customer Support AI Chatbot for an E-commerce Website"

Step 2: Define Agent Capabilities

Clearly outline what the AI agent should do.
For example, a **Customer Support AI Chatbot** should:

Handle **frequent customer queries** (e.g., order tracking, refund policies)
Provide **personalized recommendations** based on user purchase history
Detect and escalate **complex issues** to human agents
Support **multi-channel interactions** (website chat, WhatsApp, Messenger)

Step 3: Choose the AI Technology Stack

Define the tools and frameworks you will use:

Component	Technology Stack	Justification
LLM Engine	OpenAI GPT-4, LLama-3	NLP for understanding customer queries
Framework	LangChain, Rasa	Conversational AI pipelines
Database	PostgreSQL, MongoDB	Store user interactions and history
Deployment	AWS Lambda, Firebase	Cloud-based, scalable execution
Security	OAuth 2.0, JWT	Secure user authentication

Step 4: Create the AI Agent's Workflow

Define how the agent processes user input.

Example Workflow for a Customer Support Chatbot

1. **User Query Processing**
   - Extract intent (e.g., "Where is my order?")
   - Identify entities (e.g., "Order #12345")
2. **Database Lookup**
   - Fetch order details from the database
   - Retrieve expected delivery date
3. **AI Response Generation**
   - Generate a human-like response using **GPT-4**
   - Format response for clarity
4. **User Interaction & Follow-up**
   - If a follow-up question is detected, continue the conversation
   - Escalate to a human agent if needed

Example API Flow

python

```
from langchain.chat_models import ChatOpenAI

from langchain.schema import HumanMessage


chatbot = ChatOpenAI(model="gpt-4")
```

```
query = HumanMessage(content="Where is my order #12345?")

response = chatbot([query])


print(response.content)
```

Step 5: Handle Security & Privacy

Define how the agent securely manages user data.

Encryption for sensitive data (e.g., AES-256 for order details)
Authentication using JWT or OAuth for verifying user identity
Logging & Monitoring to detect abuse and prevent fraud

Step 6: Deployment Plan

Define where and how the agent will be deployed.

Component	Cloud Service	Justification
API Hosting	AWS Lambda, GCP Cloud Run	Serverless, auto-scaling
Database	PostgreSQL (AWS RDS)	Secure data storage
Monitoring	Datadog, AWS CloudWatch	Real-time performance tracking

Step 7: Evaluate Agent Performance

After deployment, measure how well the agent performs.

Key Metrics for Customer Support AI:

- **Response Time** (Goal: < 1 second)
- **Resolution Rate** (Goal: > 90% of queries resolved)

- **Customer Satisfaction (CSAT)** (Goal: > 4.5/5)

Deliverable: Document Your Design Choices

Now, summarize your AI agent's design in a structured format:

1. Use Case:

AI Chatbot for E-commerce Customer Support

2. Key Capabilities:

Order tracking, refund policies, personalized recommendations

3. Technology Stack:

GPT-4, LangChain, AWS Lambda, PostgreSQL

4. Workflow:

NLP → Database Query → AI Response → User Interaction

5. Security Considerations:

Data encryption, OAuth authentication, API rate limits

6. Deployment Plan:

Serverless architecture with AWS Lambda & Firebase

7. Performance Metrics:

Response time <1s, Resolution rate >90%, CSAT >4.5

Select an industry
Design an AI agent
Document key design choices

Now, implement your AI agent and test its performance!

Chapter 13: Emerging Trends and Future Directions

13.1 No-Code/Low-Code Development for AI Agents

No-code and low-code platforms are transforming AI agent development by enabling non-technical users and businesses to create and deploy AI-powered solutions with minimal programming knowledge. These platforms provide **drag-and-drop interfaces**, **pre-built AI models**, and **integrations with external services**, making AI more accessible.

Key Differences Between No-Code and Low-Code

Feature	No-Code AI	Low-Code AI
Target Users	Business users, non-developers	Developers, technical users
Customization	Limited (pre-built workflows)	High (custom scripting possible)
Coding Required?	No coding required	Minimal coding required
Examples	ChatGPT API on Zapier, Bubble.io, Make.com	LangChain with Flowise, Power Automate AI

No-Code AI Platforms for Agent Development

No-code platforms allow users to build AI agents using intuitive interfaces. Below are some leading platforms:

Platform	Key Features	Best For
Zapier AI	Connects LLMs with apps, automates workflows	Business automation
Bubble.io	Drag-and-drop app builder with AI plugins	AI-powered web apps
Make.com	Visual workflow automation for AI services	Customer support automation
Pipedream	No-code API integrations with AI	Serverless AI workflows

Example: Building a ChatGPT Customer Support Bot in Zapier

1. **Trigger:** New customer query in Gmail
2. **Action 1:** Send query to OpenAI GPT API
3. **Action 2:** Send AI-generated response back to email
4. **Action 3 (Optional):** Log conversation in Google Sheets

No coding required—just set up the flow visually!

Low-Code AI Platforms for Agent Development

Low-code platforms provide more customization while still simplifying AI development.

Platform	Key Features	Best For
Flowise AI	Low-code LangChain GUI for LLM workflows	AI-powered chatbots
Power Automate AI	Automates enterprise AI workflows	Business process automation
Rasa X	Low-code chatbot framework with UI	Enterprise AI assistants
Azure AI Studio	Visual AI model training & deployment	AI application development

Example: Building an AI Chatbot with Flowise

1. **Select a Pre-Trained LLM (e.g., OpenAI, Claude, LLaMA)**
2. **Define Agent Flow using Drag-and-Drop Nodes**
3. **Customize Business Logic using JavaScript**
4. **Deploy AI Bot via API or UI Embed**

Flowise bridges the gap between low-code and full-code AI agent development.

Advantages of No-Code/Low-Code AI Agent Development

Faster Time-to-Market – Develop AI solutions quickly without complex coding
Cost-Efficiency – Reduce the need for expensive AI engineers
Accessibility – Allows business teams to deploy AI without tech expertise
Scalability – Integrate with existing enterprise workflows

Challenges and Limitations

Limited Customization – No-code solutions are less flexible than full-code approaches
Security Concerns – AI agents may expose sensitive data if misconfigured
Vendor Lock-In – Reliance on platform-specific integrations may limit portability

---

Future Trends in No-Code/Low-Code AI Development

. **AI-Augmented No-Code Platforms** – AI auto-generates workflows based on descriptions
. **Integration with AutoML** – Platforms will offer easy access to custom model training
. **Multi-Agent Orchestration** – Drag-and-drop AI agents working in teams

---

No-code and low-code platforms are democratizing AI agent development. While they offer rapid prototyping and ease of use, they also come with limitations in flexibility. The future will likely bring **hybrid solutions** combining **no-code simplicity with low-code customization**.

Exercise: Build a No-Code or Low-Code AI Agent

Choose a **no-code** or **low-code** platform
Define a **real-world use case** (e.g., AI chatbot, automation bot)
Build an AI agent and **document your workflow**

Your mission: Prototype an AI agent in under 30 minutes!

13.2 Predictive Capabilities and Proactive Problem-Solving in AI Agents

Introduction

Modern AI agents are evolving beyond reactive responses; they now incorporate **predictive capabilities** and **proactive problem-solving** to enhance decision-making, optimize workflows, and improve user experiences. By leveraging **machine learning (ML), reinforcement learning (RL), and historical data analysis**, AI agents can **anticipate future outcomes** and **act before problems arise**.

What Are Predictive Capabilities?

Predictive AI agents use **historical data, machine learning models, and statistical techniques** to make **informed forecasts about future events**. These capabilities enable AI agents to:

- **Detect patterns** in large datasets
- **Forecast future trends** (e.g., customer behavior, system failures)
- **Identify risks and anomalies** before they escalate
- **Recommend proactive actions** to mitigate issues

Example: Predictive AI in Customer Support

A customer support AI agent **analyzes past interactions** and **predicts customer issues** before they happen.

- **Prediction:** Customer might cancel a subscription due to frequent issues
- **Proactive Response:** AI offers a **personalized discount or solution** before the customer reaches out

Result: Improved customer retention and satisfaction!

Key Technologies Behind Predictive AI

Technology	How It Enables Prediction	Example Use Case
Machine Learning (ML)	Learns from past data to predict future outcomes	Sales forecasting
Reinforcement Learning (RL)	Optimizes decisions by learning from trial-and-error	AI-driven trading bots
Natural Language Processing (NLP)	Analyzes text to predict sentiment or intent	Proactive chatbot responses
Time-Series Analysis	Detects trends over time for forecasting	Predictive maintenance
Anomaly Detection	Identifies unusual patterns in data	Fraud prevention

Proactive Problem-Solving in AI Agents

Unlike reactive AI, **proactive AI agents take action before an issue occurs**. They **monitor data, assess risks, and implement preventive solutions**.

How Proactive AI Works

1. **Data Collection:** AI continuously gathers data from users, systems, and sensors
2. **Pattern Recognition:** Detects early signs of potential issues
3. **Risk Assessment:** Evaluates the probability and impact of an issue
4. **Action Implementation:** Takes proactive steps to prevent problems

Example: AI in IT Operations (AIOps)

- **Monitoring:** AI analyzes server logs and detects an **increasing CPU usage trend**
- **Prediction:** Identifies a **high risk of system failure** within 48 hours
- **Proactive Solution: Auto-scales resources** before a crash occurs

Result: Prevents downtime, saving costs and improving system reliability!

Case Studies of Predictive & Proactive AI

Industry	Predictive AI Use Case	Proactive Solution
Healthcare	AI predicts **patient readmission risks**	Alerts doctors for preventive care
Finance	AI detects **fraudulent transactions** before they happen	Blocks suspicious activity automatically
E-commerce	AI predicts **customer churn**	Offers retention discounts proactively
Manufacturing	AI forecasts **machine failures**	Triggers maintenance before breakdown
Cybersecurity	AI detects **potential security threats**	Applies patches automatically

Advantages of Predictive & Proactive AI

Prevents Issues Before They Escalate – Avoids costly failures
Improves Decision-Making – Provides actionable insights in advance
Enhances User Experience – Personalized recommendations increase engagement
Optimizes Resource Allocation – AI predicts demand and adjusts resources accordingly
Reduces Operational Costs – Preventative actions minimize downtime and waste

Challenges & Limitations

Data Dependency – High-quality, large datasets are required for accurate predictions
Complexity in Implementation – Requires integration with multiple data sources
False Positives – Over-predicting risks may lead to unnecessary interventions
Ethical Concerns – Privacy issues arise when predicting user behavior

Future Trends in Predictive AI

. **AI-Driven Self-Healing Systems** – Automatically detect and fix issues in IT infrastructure
. **Proactive AI Assistants** – AI agents that predict user needs and take action before being asked
. **Hybrid Human-AI Decision-Making** – AI provides recommendations, and humans make final calls
. **AI for Crisis Management** – Predicts global crises (e.g., pandemics, economic downturns)

AI agents with **predictive capabilities** and **proactive problem-solving** are revolutionizing industries by **reducing risks, enhancing decision-making, and improving efficiency**. The future of AI lies in **anticipating problems before they occur** and **taking intelligent actions** to optimize outcomes.

Exercise: Implement Predictive AI in Your Agent

Choose a **use case** (e.g., predictive maintenance, fraud detection)
Train an AI model on **historical data** to make **predictions**
Design a **proactive response mechanism** for issue prevention
Evaluate the **effectiveness of predictions** and document findings

Your mission: Create an AI agent that can anticipate problems and take preventive action!

13.3 Multi-Modal and Emotional Intelligence in AI Agents

AI agents are evolving beyond text-based interactions to **multi-modal intelligence**, incorporating **text, speech, images, video, and sensor data** for richer communication. Additionally, **emotional intelligence (EI)** enables AI to **detect, interpret, and respond to human emotions**, making interactions more **human-like, empathetic, and effective**.

What is Multi-Modal AI?

Multi-modal AI processes and integrates **multiple types of input**, such as:

- **Text** (e.g., chat, documents)
- **Speech** (e.g., voice assistants)
- **Images** (e.g., facial recognition)
- **Videos** (e.g., surveillance analysis)
- **Sensor Data** (e.g., IoT monitoring)

Example: Multi-Modal AI in Virtual Assistants

A smart assistant **combines text, voice, and visual data** to **provide better responses**:

- **User:** *"How's the weather?"*
- AI **detects location** via GPS
- AI **uses speech synthesis** to reply: *"It's sunny in your area with 75°F."*
- AI **displays real-time radar images** of the weather forecast

Result: A seamless, natural, and richer user experience!

How Multi-Modal AI Works

1. **Data Fusion:** AI **collects input** from multiple sources
2. **Processing:** Different AI models (e.g., NLP for text, CNNs for images) analyze the data
3. **Integration:** AI combines insights from various modalities
4. **Response Generation:** AI formulates the best output based on **combined inputs**

Example: AI in Healthcare

- 👀 AI **analyzes patient facial expressions** to detect pain levels
- AI **processes patient speech** for stress indicators
- . AI **examines medical images** (X-rays, MRIs) for anomalies
- AI **compares patient history** to detect potential diseases

Result: Faster, more accurate medical diagnoses!

What is Emotional Intelligence in AI?

Emotional Intelligence (EI) in AI refers to the **ability to recognize, interpret, and respond to human emotions**. It enhances AI by enabling:

- **Emotion Detection** – Identifying sentiment from text, speech, and facial expressions
- **Context-Aware Responses** – Adjusting communication style based on emotions
- **Empathetic Interaction** – Simulating human-like emotional engagement

Example: Emotionally Aware AI in Customer Support

- AI detects **customer frustration** from voice tone
- AI **prioritizes urgent resolution** for dissatisfied users
- AI **adjusts tone** (e.g., apologetic for complaints, cheerful for greetings)
- . AI **proactively offers solutions** to defuse tension

Result: Increased customer satisfaction and better human-AI interaction!

Technologies Behind Multi-Modal and Emotional AI

Technology	Function	Example Use Case
Natural Language Processing (NLP)	Understands and processes text	AI chatbots, virtual assistants
Speech Recognition	Converts speech to text	Voice assistants (e.g., Siri, Alexa)
Computer Vision (CV)	Analyzes images and facial expressions	AI emotion detection

Technology	Function	Example Use Case
Sentiment Analysis	Detects emotions in text/speech	Social media monitoring
Multi-Modal Transformers (e.g., CLIP, Flamingo)	Combines text, images, and audio for better understanding	AI-powered search engines
Affective Computing	Simulates human emotions in AI responses	Virtual therapists

Case Studies of Multi-Modal and Emotional AI

Industry	Multi-Modal AI Use Case	Emotional Intelligence AI Use Case
Healthcare	AI analyzes medical scans & patient speech for diagnostics	AI detects stress in a patient's voice & adjusts tone
Customer Service	AI processes chat, voice, and video for better support	AI detects anger & escalates issue to a human
Retail	AI suggests fashion products based on user images	AI gauges shopper sentiment via facial expressions
Automotive	AI monitors driver eye movements & voice for fatigue	AI adapts car assistant voice based on driver mood
Education	AI integrates speech, handwriting & text for personalized learning	AI adjusts teaching pace based on student frustration

Advantages of Multi-Modal & Emotional AI

Improved User Engagement – AI interactions feel more **human-like**
Better Accuracy in Understanding Context – AI interprets **multiple inputs together**
Enhanced Personalization – AI adapts to **user preferences and emotions**
Higher Customer Satisfaction – AI detects frustration and **proactively offers solutions**

More Inclusive AI – AI supports **voice, text, images, and gestures** for accessibility

---

Challenges & Limitations

Data Complexity – Requires large, **high-quality** multi-modal datasets
Bias Risks – Emotional detection models may misinterpret **cultural differences**
Processing Overhead – Handling multiple inputs requires **higher computing power**
Privacy Concerns – AI collecting facial expressions & voice data raises **ethical issues**

Future Trends in Multi-Modal and Emotional AI

. **Emotionally Adaptive AI Agents** – AI that adjusts **tone, voice, and expressions** dynamically
. **AI with Visual and Contextual Awareness** – AI assistants that **see and understand** real-world environments
. **Multi-Modal Conversational AI** – AI that **seamlessly integrates speech, gestures, and text** for interactions
. **AI-Powered Therapy Bots** – Emotionally intelligent AI for **mental health support**
. **Augmented Reality (AR) & AI Fusion** – AI-powered AR that **interprets gestures and emotions** in real-time

---

Multi-modal and emotionally intelligent AI agents are **reshaping human-computer interaction** by **understanding context, emotions, and multiple data types**. These capabilities **enhance personalization, improve decision-making, and create seamless experiences** in customer service, healthcare, education, and more.

The future of AI lies in combining intelligence with emotional understanding!

Exercise: Build a Multi-Modal AI Agent with Emotional Intelligence

Choose a **use case** (e.g., healthcare, education, customer service)
Integrate **multi-modal inputs** (text, voice, images, or video)
Implement **emotion detection** using **sentiment analysis & facial recognition**
Design an AI **response strategy** that adapts to user emotions
Test and document how the AI **improves user engagement & interaction**

Your challenge: Develop an AI agent that understands and responds to emotions!

13.4 Other Emerging Trends: Agent Orchestration, Decentralized AI, and Beyond

AI agents are rapidly evolving, integrating new paradigms such as **agent orchestration** and **decentralized AI** to enhance efficiency, autonomy, and scalability. These trends are **redefining how AI systems collaborate, process data, and operate across networks**.

---

1. Agent Orchestration: Coordinating AI Agents for Complex Tasks

What is Agent Orchestration?

Agent orchestration refers to the **coordinated management of multiple AI agents** to achieve complex goals. It involves:

- **Task delegation** – Assigning specialized tasks to different agents
- **Workflow automation** – Structuring agent interactions for seamless execution
- **Decision coordination** – Ensuring agents collaborate efficiently

Example: AI-Powered Business Process Automation

A company integrates AI agents to **streamline customer support**:

1. **Agent 1:** Monitors incoming customer queries
2. **Agent 2:** Analyzes sentiment & urgency
3. **Agent 3:** Suggests solutions or escalates issues
4. **Agent 4:** Automates follow-ups

Result: Faster response times, improved efficiency, and enhanced customer experience!

Technologies Enabling Agent Orchestration

Technology	Function	Example Use Case
LangGraph / CrewAI	Multi-agent workflow coordination	AI-powered assistants
Graph Neural Networks (GNNs)	Optimizing agent communication	AI for logistics planning
Reinforcement Learning (RL)	Optimizing agent decision-making	AI-based supply chain automation
LLM-based Planning	AI-driven strategic task execution	Automated research agents

2. Decentralized AI: The Future of AI Autonomy

What is Decentralized AI?

Decentralized AI **distributes computing power and decision-making** across multiple nodes instead of relying on centralized servers. This enhances:

- **Privacy & Security** – No single point of failure
- **Scalability** – AI operates efficiently across networks
- **Resilience** – AI continues functioning even if some nodes fail

Example: AI in Blockchain-Powered Smart Contracts

A **blockchain-based AI system** manages **automated loan approvals**:

1. **Node 1:** Verifies user identity
2. **Node 2:** Assesses creditworthiness

3. **Node 3:** Processes loan approval securely

Result: Transparent, trustless, and tamper-proof AI-driven finance!

Technologies Enabling Decentralized AI

Technology	Function	Example Use Case
Blockchain	Ensures trust & security in AI interactions	AI-driven financial contracts
Federated Learning	AI training across distributed networks	Privacy-preserving healthcare AI
Swarm Intelligence	Decentralized decision-making	AI-driven supply chain optimization
Edge AI	Processing AI at local devices instead of the cloud	AI-powered IoT (smart homes, smart cities)

3. AI-Powered Autonomous Systems

What are Autonomous AI Systems?

These are AI-driven systems that **self-optimize, adapt to changes, and operate without human intervention**.

- **Self-driving cars** adapt to **real-time road conditions**
- **AI in manufacturing** adjusts workflows **based on production efficiency**
- **AI in healthcare** detects **early disease symptoms**

Result: Fully automated, self-sufficient AI applications!

4. AI-Augmented Creativity & Human-AI Collaboration

What is AI-Augmented Creativity?

AI is **enhancing human creativity** by generating ideas, artwork, music, and even code:

- **AI-assisted design** (e.g., AI-generated architecture)
- **AI-powered storytelling** (e.g., AI-driven book writing)
- **AI-enhanced music composition** (e.g., AI-generated symphonies)

Example: AI in Game Development

AI-powered tools assist developers by:

- Generating **realistic environments**
- Creating **dynamic storylines**
- Enhancing **non-player character (NPC) behavior**

Result: More immersive and dynamic gaming experiences!

Case Studies of Emerging AI Trends

Trend	Example Use Case	Impact
Agent Orchestration	AI-powered research assistants collaborating	Faster, multi-perspective insights
Decentralized AI	Blockchain-based AI for fraud detection	Secure and tamper-proof decision-making
Autonomous AI Systems	AI-driven traffic management	Reduced congestion, improved road safety
AI-Augmented Creativity	AI-powered music & art generation	Expands creative possibilities

Advantages of Emerging AI Trends

Enhanced Efficiency – AI automates & optimizes workflows
Greater Privacy & Security – Decentralized AI protects data
Scalability – Distributed AI solutions work across large networks
Improved Collaboration – AI agents work together for better outcomes
Increased Creativity – AI enhances human-generated content

Challenges & Limitations

Complexity in Implementation – Requires **specialized infrastructure**
Computational Costs – AI orchestration & decentralization need **high processing power**
Ethical Concerns – Autonomous AI **must align with human values**
Lack of Standardization – New AI paradigms **lack clear regulations**

Future Trends in AI

. **Self-Learning AI Agents** – AI that **improves autonomously over time**
. **Hybrid Human-AI Teams** – AI working alongside **humans for decision-making**
. **Explainable AI (XAI)** – AI that **transparently explains its decisions**
. **Quantum AI** – AI leveraging **quantum computing for super-fast processing**

The future of AI lies in **agent orchestration, decentralized intelligence, autonomous decision-making, and AI-augmented creativity**. These technologies **expand AI's potential, making systems more adaptable, collaborative, and secure.**

AI is no longer just a tool – it's becoming an intelligent, networked ecosystem!

Exercise: Explore an Emerging AI Trend

Pick a **trend** (e.g., agent orchestration, decentralized AI, autonomous systems)
Design a **concept AI agent** leveraging this trend
Implement a **basic prototype** (if possible)
Document **how it improves efficiency, security, or decision-making**

Your challenge: Build an AI agent that embraces the future of AI!

Exercise 13.5: Explore an Emerging AI Trend and Propose a Future Application

Objective

In this exercise, you will explore an **emerging trend in AI agent development**, analyze its potential, and propose a **future application** that leverages this trend. Your goal is to identify an **innovative, real-world use case** where AI can provide **a significant impact**.

Step 1: Choose an Emerging AI Trend

Select one of the **emerging trends** in AI, such as:

- **Agent Orchestration** – Coordinating multiple AI agents for complex tasks
- **Decentralized AI** – Using blockchain or federated learning to enable secure AI networks
- **Autonomous AI Systems** – AI that self-improves and operates independently
- **AI-Augmented Creativity** – AI that enhances human-generated content
- **Explainable AI (XAI)** – AI systems that provide transparent and interpretable decisions
- **Quantum AI** – Leveraging quantum computing for AI acceleration

---

. Step 2: Research the Chosen Trend

- **How does it work?** (Describe the key concepts behind this trend)
- **What are its current applications?** (Provide real-world examples of how this technology is being used)
- **What challenges does it face?** (Discuss limitations or barriers to adoption)

Step 3: Propose a Future AI Application

Design a **new, innovative application** leveraging your chosen trend.
Consider:

- **Problem Statement:** What issue does this AI solve?
- **Technology Stack:** What tools, frameworks, or infrastructure are needed?
- **How AI is Used:** How does AI enhance or automate the process?
- **Expected Impact:** What benefits does this AI bring to users, industries, or society?

Example Proposal: AI-Powered Personalized Healthcare System

Trend Chosen: Decentralized AI + Federated Learning

Problem: Traditional healthcare AI models lack patient privacy and data security due to centralized processing.

Proposed Solution: A blockchain-powered federated learning system that enables hospitals and research institutions to collaborate on AI models without sharing raw patient data.

How AI is Used:

AI learns from **decentralized datasets** across hospitals, ensuring **patient privacy**
Uses **personalized AI recommendations** for early disease detection
Blockchain secures data transactions and model updates

Expected Impact:

Improved **patient data security**
Faster **medical research breakthroughs**
AI-assisted diagnosis with greater accuracy

. Step 4: Document Your Findings

Prepare a **summary** of your research and proposal:

1. **Trend Overview** – Explain your chosen AI trend
2. **Current Applications** – Where is this technology being used today?
3. **Challenges** – What are the barriers to adoption?
4. **Future AI Application Proposal** – Describe your innovation
5. **Potential Benefits** – How will your AI solution impact the world?

. **Bonus Challenge**

- Sketch a **basic architecture diagram** for your AI system
- Identify **potential ethical concerns** (e.g., bias, security risks, misuse)
- Think about **how your AI system could evolve in the next 5-10 years**

Now it's your turn! Explore, innovate, and design the future of AI!

www.ingramcontent.com/pod-product-compliance
Lightning Source LLC
LaVergne TN
LVHW080113070326
832902LV00015B/2554